Praise for the Author

"Throughout everyone's competition career there is the niggling question of what does the judge want? What is going on on the other side of the clipboard and scorecard? This splendid book by Joanne Verikios answers our questions and sets us on the road to success in competition and out of it!" **Jeanne O'Malley, Author of** *Training the Performance Horse* **and** *Riding in Mounted Games*.

"*Winning Horsemanship* is a clear winner for both horse and rider/handler. It offers powerful insight into the equine thought process and their behaviour, as well as strong motivation to the rider/handler. This is truly a 'thinking horseman's' book, for those who want to build a lasting and successful partnership with their equine counterparts. What I love most about this book is that it offers a holistic approach to both horse and rider, with empathy and compassion shown for the horses." **Claudette Johnson, Beau Cheval Warmblood Stud, AWHA Ltd Federal President.**

"As a business coach and strategist, I love any preparation that gives you an edge over your competitors. And that's exactly what this book does. It doesn't matter if you just want to take care of the horse you love, or be competitive to win Equestrian Gold at the Olympic Games or ride the Melbourne Cup winner; it's all within your reach if you adopt the principles and tips included in *Winning Horsemanship*. You cannot help but benefit from the wisdom, experience and successes of Joanne Verikios. This book is for people who care about their horse, care about improving their relationship with their horse and also improving the competitive outcome. It's solid gold." **Mark Brigden, Author of** *Become A Game Changer*.

"*Winning Horsemanship* is easy to read, full of gems of wisdom and illustrative anecdotes. Whether you are new to competing with your horse or have been doing so for a while, whatever your field of interest, this book will have something for you." **Andrea Fleming, owner and rider of Thoroughbreds, Australian Stock Horses, Warmbloods and Standardbreds.**

"Deciding to swap a tractor for a horse felt like a good decision. Spontaneous and logical because we could not master driving a tractor and we are blessed with great respect and love for animals. Absolute beginners and teachers by profession we turned to literature on horses, also logical. This book is a unique combination of personal and professional experiences and it addressed and filled our thirst for not only information but knowledge as well. I now feel confident that we can and will master this glorious skill of horse-human relationship. *Winning Horsemanship* bridges the gap between human weakness and equine strength. I would recommend it not only to beginners but to everyone who loves horses and definitely to those who keep them or are considering that option. Buy it for the horse lovers in your life and be sure to read it yourself." **Dragana Boljesic, First Time Owner of an American Paint Horse, Croatia.**

"A must read for anyone interested in knowing more about horses and the relationship you should develop with your horse. Great coverage, pulling together the wide-ranging aspects of horsemanship into one book. Having been involved with horses for over forty years, I was pleased to learn new things as well as refreshing my knowledge and thinking of new ways of working with my horses. I particularly liked the reflections on the foundations of good horsemanship which are unrelated to whichever discipline you are interested in, but rather about the special bond you establish with your horse. This book reflects on the many ways we should think about winning, especially the elements of leadership and trust that are so important and valuable as to how we interact with horses. I enjoyed this book and found it an easy read while being very informative. The cameos from so many different horse people from such diverse equestrian disciplines were particularly interesting and educative. Well done – it will be the perfect gift." **Jaclyne Fisher, Dressage Rider, Stud Manager, Importer and Breeder of Warmblood Horses.**

"With only limited personal experience in the equine world, I approached *Winning Horsemanship* with some hesitation. Yet the book managed not only to expand my appreciation of these magnificent creatures, but also shine a light on the skills we need to be better human beings." **Ian Grayson, Freelance Journalist.**

Praise for the Author

"Delightful reading for both amateurs and professionals alike, *Winning Horsemanship* incites introspective reflection and motivation, sending the reader on a journey to self-betterment both as an individual and as a horse person. *Winning Horsemanship* is a wonderful insight into the values of a trusting partnership including the trials, tribulations, commitment, elation and joy of horse ownership. The author captures the imagination and soul of the reader and reinvigorates the childhood passion we have for our horses." **Shanna Antrim, Proprietor, Harris Park Warmbloods, AWHA Ltd Publicity Officer.**

WINNING HORSEMANSHIP

Global Publishing Group
Australia • New Zealand • Singapore • America • London

WINNING HORSEMANSHIP

A Judge's Secrets And Tips For Your Success

JOANNE VERIKIOS

DISCLAIMER

All the information, techniques, skills and concepts contained within this publication are of the nature of general comment only and are not in any way recommended as individual advice. The intent is to offer a variety of information to provide a wider range of choices now and in the future, recognising that we all have widely diverse circumstances and viewpoints. Should any reader choose to make use of the information contained herein, this is their decision, and the contributors (and their companies), authors and publishers do not assume any responsibilities whatsoever under any condition or circumstances. It is recommended that the reader obtain their own independent advice.

First Edition 2016

Copyright © 2016 Joanne Verikios

All rights are reserved. The material contained within this book is protected by copyright law, no part may be copied, reproduced, presented, stored, communicated or transmitted in any form by any means without prior written permission..

National Library of Australia
Cataloguing-in-Publication entry:

Creator: Verikios, Joanne, author.

Winning Horsemanship : A Judge's Secrets and Tips For Your Success / Joanne Verikios.

1st ed.
ISBN: 9781925288001 (paperback)

Horsemanship.
Horsemanship – Coaching.
Horsemanship – Competitions.

Dewey Number: 798.2

Published by Global Publishing Group
PO Box 517 Mt Evelyn, Victoria 3796 Australia
Email info@GlobalPublishingGroup.com.au

For further information about orders:
Phone: +61 3 9739 4686 or Fax +61 3 8648 6871

For my parents,
with gratitude and love.

JOANNE VERIKIOS

Acknowledgements

This book would not exist without the love, tuition and patience of so many people and horses that to list them all would be a book in itself.

I will, however, make some very special mentions. Heartfelt thanks to my wonderful husband, George Verikios, and to my parents, Joan and Trev Liesegang, who epitomise a life lived with honour, integrity and kindness.

Thank you to my brother, Stephen Liesegang, and my sister, Brenda Papworth, for inspiring me with your artistic achievements; and to my grandparents, extended family and friends who have been a powerful source of guidance and accountability.

The men and women who have influenced my equestrian, breeding and judging endeavours – knowingly or unknowingly – have my deep appreciation. These include Alois Podhajsky, Angus McKinnon, Anna Sewell, Bart Cummings, Bev Edwards, Bill Roycroft, Buck Brannaman, Charles Chipp, Clemens Dierks, Dirk Dijkstra, Edgar Lichtwark, Franz Mairinger, Fred Hoevenaars, Gary Dowling, Holger Schmorl, J.D. Wilton, Jack Laing, Klaus Balkenhol, Les Watterson, Lucinda Green, Mary Wanless, Maurice Wright, M.I. Clarke, Mike Fagan, Nuno Oliveira, Pat and Linda Parelli, Phil Rodey, HRH Princess Anne, HRH Queen Elizabeth II, Reiner Klimke, Richard L. Wätjen, Richard Weis, Sally Swift, Scott Tucker, Vince Corvi and Wayne Roycroft. In particular, I would like to thank Jack Pappas, without whom the Highborn Warmblood Stud would not have been possible.

I also thank the Downs Pony Club, especially Miss Janine Turner and Miss Silvia Manning; the Cumburrie Trail Horse Riding Club, especially R.M. Williams; the National Capital Horse Trials Association and the Australian Warmblood Horse Association Ltd.

Lynne Crowden, thank you for your contribution to the international horse scene, your fellowship as a judge, and for honouring my book with your thoughtful Foreword.

To Andrea Fleming, Camilla Davis, Chris Christoff, Christopher Ardron, Claudette Johnson, Dragana Boljesic, Ian Grayson, Ian King, Jaci Fisher, Jeanne O'Malley, Jude Matusiewicz, Katie Umback, Maija McLoughlin, Mark Brigden, Shanna Antrim, Silvia Ahamer and Suzy Roe, thank you for your enthusiasm for my vision and for your generous assistance and unique contributions, all of which have shaped and improved this book.

I gratefully acknowledge the brilliant team at Global Publishing Group for their belief in my project and for guiding it to conclusion. Particular thanks go to marketing genius, Darren Stephens; resident equine expert, Jackie Tallentyre; and the very talented Kelly Mayne.

Mickaela Grace, Kurt Iwanina and Simone de Haas, thank you for helping me to find my voice.

I would also like to acknowledge the teachers, friends and mentors who have contributed to my own development as a teacher, friend and mentor. These include Professor Boris Christa, Brendan Kelly, Brendan Nichols, Chris Hector, Dr Christiane Northrup, Darren Hardy, Dr Denis Waitley, Earl Nightingale, Jim Rohn, Dr Kathleen Simmons, Kurek Ashley, Louise Hay, Margaret Price, Michael Rowland, Dr Myron Wentz, Pat Mesiti, Sharan Kafoa, Stephen Covey, Steven Pressfield and Suzanne Rix.

Last, but by no means least, to Star, Beauty, Bimbo, Cloud, Zyla, Rusty, Duco and Powerlifter – thank you for the joy and the lessons, you live in my heart.

Joanne Verikios

Contents

Foreword by Lynne Crowden		**1**
Introduction		**3**
Chapter 1:	Beginnings	**7**
Chapter 2:	Acquire	**19**
Chapter 3:	Nourish	**33**
Chapter 4:	Nurture	**49**
Chapter 5:	Condition	**65**
Chapter 6:	Educate	**81**
Chapter 7:	Teaching to Learn	**93**
Chapter 8:	Prepare	**109**
Chapter 9:	Becoming a Champion	**119**
Chapter 10:	Groundwork	**129**
Chapter 11:	Teamwork	**143**
Chapter 12:	The Psychology of Confidence	**157**
Chapter 13:	Present – It's Showtime	**169**
Author's Final Word		**183**
About the Author		**185**
Recommended Resources		**187**

EXTRA BONUSES!
Valued at over $250.00 but Yours FREE!

Success-Enhancing Products from Winning Horsemanship™

Claim your FREE downloads by going to www.WinningHorsemanship.com/gifts

- **BONUS #1** Winning Horsemanship Companion Workbook

  Essential follow-through tools for your ongoing accountability, inspiration and motivation. Discover actions for success that mirror the book chapter-by-chapter. Bring new balance and fulfilment to your horsemanship, your mindset and your life.

- **BONUS #2** Health for Horse Owners

  Bonus chapter! This wouldn't fit in the book but I want you to have it!

- **BONUS #3** Equine Learning

  Exclusive recording and transcript of the full interview with Maija McLoughlin, horse handler extraordinaire. Read the text or listen to the audio!

- **BONUS #4** Goal Setting

  Exclusive recording and transcript of the full interview with Chris Christoff, author of Goal Setting for People Who Can't Set Goals. Read the text or listen to the audio!

- **BONUS #5** On Horsemanship by Xenophon

  Your own copy of the first ever manual on selecting and training horses – in handy eBook format.

- **BONUS #6** e-Poster courtesy of Evidence Based Worming

  Lifecycle of a Cyathostomin (Small Strongyle). Not just a lifecycle diagram, this attractive poster contains many fascinating facts and insights about Cyathostomins, in colour and fully referenced. Perfect for your study or tack room wall.

Claim your FREE BONUS GIFTS NOW by going to www.WinningHorsemanship.com/gifts

Foreword

The spirit, natural grace and generosity of the horse have always been the inspiration behind my own equestrian pursuits of breeding and training horses for Olympic disciplines and other equestrian sport, including hunting and racing. The essence of the relationship between the horse and the rider or handler lies in respect, but also knowledge and care.

Our goal is to produce exceptional sport horses; the key is getting the basics right. For over twenty years at Woodlander Stud, my husband Dave and I have bred top competition horses from German mares. To date, the absolute highlight was an outstanding win for the homebred Woodlander Farouche in the five-year old World Championship in Verden, Germany in 2011, a win which would be repeated in 2012 when Farouche added the six-year-old World Championship to her résumé. Hearing the judges unable to speak of anything else but this incredible horse was one of the proudest moments of my life!

Dave and I have bred nearly five hundred foals, over a hundred affiliated dressage horses and fourteen approved stallions, and to ensure we achieve the best results we have worked with the best trainers and riders, including Michael Beining, Danny Pevsner, Carl Hester and latterly Michael Eilberg. I am committed to the improvement of the breed worldwide but also work hard to promote British Breeding, the British Bred Sport Horse, British Breeders' Network, the Warmblood Breeders' Studbook UK and the British Hanoverian Horse Society.

I met the author of this book, Joanne Verikios, in 2014 when she and I were invited to officiate as judges for the inaugural National Assessment Tour conducted by the Australian Warmblood Horse Association.

Like me, Joanne emphasises the dual importance of establishing the basics and striving for excellence. Communication is the key, understanding is everything, action based on knowledge leads to success. Joanne's long and wide experience with horses, from Pony Club to breeding a licensed stallion and standing him at stud, from feeding to foaling, from training to competing, have culminated in a book which shares the wisdom one needs to become a complete horseman. *Winning Horsemanship* not only contains invaluable tips and advice, it goes beyond mere instruction to explore the most elemental aspects of the relationship between humans and horses. Joanne's passion for empowering horsemen and horsewomen to provide their horses with a better deal while furthering their own goals is refreshing.

As with any worthwhile endeavour, there will undoubtedly be moments of frustration in your quest for better horsemanship and more success, but ultimately you will know you are winning when the dialogue between you and your horse is seamless and imperceptible, more of a whisper than a headline.

No matter what winning means to you, I hope that this book inspires you to search for harmony with your horse and wish you a rewarding and happy journey.

Lynne Crowden

Introduction

> *"The horse lends you his strength, speed and grace, which are greater than yours. For your part, you give him guidance, intelligence and understanding which are greater than his. Together you can achieve a richness that neither can alone."*
>
> Lucy Rees

A horse is beautiful, tactile, powerful. It's like having a work of art, a companion and a sports car in the same package. Being a better horseman enables you to bring out all those qualities to their optimum expression, and at your bidding. Being a better horseman brings control and predictability, without suppressing the horse's innate characteristics. Being a better horseman leads to winning horsemanship.

Thank you for choosing this book. I wrote with the intention of helping to change your life and your horse's life for the better. The combination of an eye for a horse, a way with horses, many miles in the saddle, well over fifty years spent learning about horses and a lot of hard-won experience of what can go so beautifully right, what can go so horribly wrong, and everything in between, means that I can see at a glance when things are working and when they are not. I want to share those gold nuggets of information that will be of the most use to the most people, to save horse lovers and their horses from the pain of confusion and anxiety.

It's not that there is a shortage of information – in many ways there is now too much information freely available, particularly on the internet, and a lot of it is misleading or even wrong. There are also many excellent horse books. As I added to my own library over the years, I found that no matter what the topic or how many books I had on the same subject, I always learned at least one or two new things that made the price of the book and the time taken to read it more than worthwhile. My goal for this book is to give you as many such gifts as possible, whether they be reminders, 'aha' moments or simply the comfort that others have experienced the same problems as you and have found a way through.

Two things inspired me to put my thoughts down on paper. One was watching a lot of people doing a pretty good job with their horses but missing a couple of key skills that would make all the difference to their performance. The other was the tragic and very public death of a beautiful horse through a set of circumstances that could have been avoided had the humans involved had more horse sense. This book is for horses as much as for horse lovers. Horses don't read books, so they rely on us for their health, happiness and sanity. They rely on us not to misuse the power we have over their lives. Building a better relationship with your horse will enhance your likelihood of success in every aspect of your life, and that is exciting.

This book is designed to cut through the hype and the clutter; to separate the wheat from the chaff. It will point you in the right direction and make it easier for you to shape your own journey to winning horsemanship, whatever that means for you. It contains many of the lessons from my own and other experts' lifelong learning about horses, wrought from good and bad instruction; from experiences that ranged from the wondrous to the devastating. It also reflects my own philosophy and wisdom, along with the knowledge gleaned from many thousands of dollars and hours invested in lessons, clinics and courses.

Introduction

Better horsemanship enhances safety and increases enjoyment for both horses and humans. It also provides a winning edge because, just as simple mistakes and seemingly minor or inconsequential issues can diminish your likelihood of success, tiny changes can exponentially increase it.

The skills and techniques you will learn from this book will set you up for success with horses, whether your passion is hacking, equitation, showing, eventing, dressage, show jumping, hunter classes, endurance riding, racing, camp drafting, pleasure riding, cutting, reining, polo, polocrosse, harness, Pony Club, stock work or breeding.

If the show ring or the Olympic dais is your goal, these skills and techniques will help you to win. If you want to help your horse to perform better in breed classes, classification or colt selection, they will give you a winning edge. If you want no more than a glorious trail ride in peace and harmony with your horse and all of nature, then that too is winning.

I am confident that, if you read this book with an open mind and an open heart, and then apply the time-honoured principles and the 'new' hints and tips, you will improve your relationship with your horse and move towards truly winning horsemanship.

> *Becoming a better horseman is the greatest thing you can do for a horse.*
>
> JOANNE VERIKIOS

chapter 1

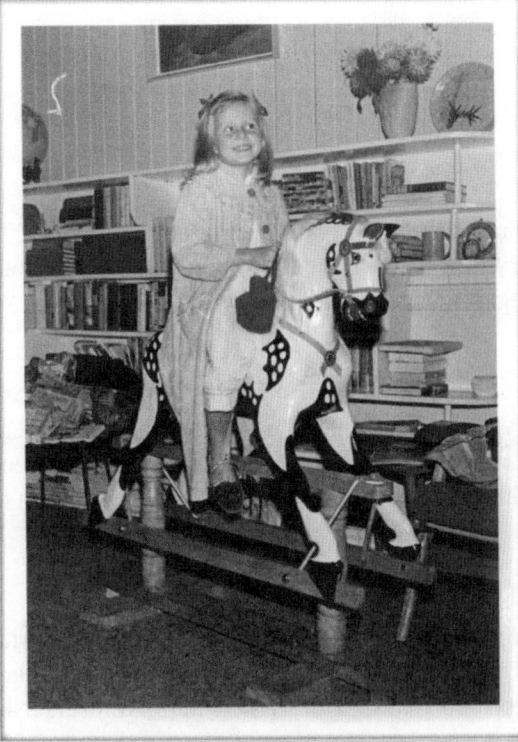

Christmas morning, 1963.
Photographer: T.W. Liesegang

BEGINNINGS

"Success isn't a result of spontaneous combustion. You must set yourself on fire."

ARNOLD H. GLASGOW

chapter 1
BEGINNINGS

Can anyone tell me how it starts, that longing for a horse? 'Why' is a beautiful mystery, but I needed a horse, had to ride, with a white-hot intensity that began as soon as I knew what a horse was; or possibly even before.

And then, those amazing, blissful moments when I got close to one – usually a shaggy pony but sometimes something more elegant. I can still feel the soft nose, with its gentle prickle of whiskers, see the liquid eyes and smell that intoxicating whiff of grassy breath from my earliest encounters.

> A high point of my young life was an unforgettable trail ride at the Gold Coast. I was only about six years old and had never had a lesson but I decided I could ride. When the organisers asked who wanted to take it easy and who wanted to go in the group that went for a longer ride and also cantered, of course I volunteered for the maximum possible time with a horse. Luckily I actually stayed on and I loved every minute of it. It was a different story for my parents, who expected to see me arrive back safe and sound with my brother and a couple of young family friends when the sedate group concluded their tour of the property. Instead, to their horror, they saw the 'advanced' group zooming along in the distance, me, with handfuls of flying mane, amongst them!

As you can imagine, my parents were very well briefed on the fact that I wanted a horse of my own. From the moment I could talk I was asking for a pony. Learning to read and write brought two major advantages. The first was that I could read books about horses. The second was that I could now pester my parents in writing. So I began to leave notes saying *"PLEASE BUY ME A PONY"* around the house.

CHAPTER 1: BEGINNINGS

In response, I received more horse books and a rocking horse.

The real breakthrough came when I recruited my father's customers to my campaign. Dad had a pharmacy, which at the time was attached to our house. It was easy for me to go into the shop and deploy my notes. I would conceal them under cakes of soap or tubes of toothpaste, but especially in the strategically important veterinary section, adjacent to the dispensary, where I knew people who loved animals would spend time selecting their purchases and talking to my father.

My horsemanship journey really began when I was about eight years old. Having found a note behind a bottle of liniment, a racehorse trainer told Dad that I could ride his lead pony, Star, when Star had finished his early morning job of escorting racehorses to Clifford Park Racetrack and back. Fortune was really smiling on me that day. First of all, the stables where Star lived were just down the road, one street behind us. Secondly, I am blessed that my benefactor, mentor and first riding instructor was Mr Les Watterson.

Mr Watterson was the jockey who rode Bernborough – the eighth greatest racehorse Australia has produced, according Aaron Hamilton in *Top Ten Australian Racehorses of All Time* (www.racingbase.com) – in his first six races for six wins back in 1941. When he took me under his wing some twenty-three years later, Mr Watterson had a small training establishment with a row of stables, a tack room, a feed room, an exercise yard at the front and turnout yards and a paddock out the back.

Toowoomba jockey and trainer, Mr Les Watterson, pictured in Mighty Bernborough *by Bill Sigley. Reproduced with permission of Boolarong Press.*

I was in heaven. Mind you, Star was by no means a child's pony. For one thing he was actually a galloway and for another he didn't approve of having his lazy afternoon routine disrupted by a pesky little girl who wanted to ride him up and down the driveway. With guidance from Mr Watterson, who was an exceptionally patient, kind and capable horseman, I soon learned how to influence Star and we got on well.

I also loved hanging around the stables, patting the racehorses, listening to Mr Watterson and his friends and, in the process, learning about feeding, grooming, doctoring, shoeing, worming and mucking out, as well as hearing all manner of stories and lore.

CHAPTER 1: BEGINNINGS

> The racehorses all had their own personalities but perhaps the strangest was a chestnut gelding nicknamed 'Tongue'. When a human approached, Tongue's ears pricked up and he would stick out his tongue.
>
> "He wants you to pull his tongue," Mr Watterson told me. Prepared for anything, I tentatively touched Tongue's tongue. He looked so pleased that I gave it a little tug. Mr Watterson was right. A bit of gentle traction on his tongue was Tongue's idea of a good time, and indulging this unusual habit soon became part of my daily routine.

Notwithstanding getting to know Mr Watterson's horses, I still clung to my dream of a pony of my own. One day, when I was nine years old, the whole family got in the car and drove to the outskirts of Toowoomba. There I met a five-year-old piebald mare called Beauty. Beauty was about twelve hands high and had done some stock work. My parents said that "we could borrow Beauty for a while" but I knew this was it – Beauty was going to be mine – my dream was coming true – I had a pony at last!

I later found out that Beauty's owner, a customer called Mr Tom Cosgrove, had said to my father, "Trevor, this is the third note I have found this month! When are you going to buy that poor kid a pony? Come out to my place this weekend and bring your wallet with you".

Thank you, Mr Watterson. Thank you, Mr Cosgrove. Thank you, Mum and Dad! Beauty was a beloved member of our family until she passed away peacefully at home in 1981.

Riding Beauty at our first Toowoomba Royal Show, 1966. I still have the red ribbon we won that day, for placing second in a class of two. Photographer unknown.

Looking back, my clarity of purpose helped me to achieve my dearest goal. I wanted a pony, with a passion that still moves me more than fifty years down the track. My quest for a pony was a metaphor for a successful life; in other words, a metaphor for winning. It is also a metaphor for winning horsemanship. I learned that:

Consistency communicates. Because I was a child, I framed my desire very simply: "Please buy me a pony".

Persistence pays. I never gave up. I simply kept making my request in person and writing my little notes, for years, until my dream came true. Creative touches like harnessing the family Labrador with a rope bridle

CHAPTER 1: BEGINNINGS

complete with a stick for a bit, and pretending to ride him, helped to reinforce my marketing.

Dreams develop. I wanted a pony, I wanted to ride. You could say I needed a pony and needed to ride, perhaps not in the same way our bodies need air, but definitely for the sustenance of my soul. You may have heard of the reticular activating system, or RAS, which helps us to focus on what we want. Well, my RAS was on high alert and I manifested what I wanted. First I rode other people's horses, then I got a pony of my own, then another pony, then… But we will touch on that later in the book.

Vision vitalises. Because my vision was so clear, I had complete confidence that I would be able to take care of my pony, ride her and succeed in whatever she and I set out to do together. No-one told me so, no-one provided constant reinforcement that it would all be alright, but there was not a shred of doubt in my mind. I knew I could do it, I knew it would work and I knew it would be wonderful. And so it was.

If the above lessons were a formula, it would be: CC + PP + DD + VV = WINNING.

My belief in my young self was total. I fell off, I got back on, and I learned and improved. I actually tried to conceal my horse-related injuries, because I didn't want my parents to think that ponies were dangerous and that Beauty might therefore have to go. If something went wrong I would always say it was my fault, never Beauty's fault. Looking back, I realise how wise that was – it is always our fault, not the horse's, as we will discuss in another chapter.

Doubts crept in later, of course, as I grew older and more "susceptible to the negative influences of other people". When this started to happen, the perfect orb in which my ponies and I existed sometimes became dented, cracked and battered by the dream-stealing conditioning that is called many names. Names like 'growing up', or 'being realistic', or 'fear of failure' or even 'what will people think?' I am sure you know what I mean.

The good news is that such conditioning can be addressed and your self-confidence can be repaired. You can build a shiny new winning mindset and you can keep it for life.

Basics

As a judge, it gives me great pleasure to note an increase in the standard of horses being bred and presented across the board. I have a particular interest in Warmbloods, and the selective breeding practices encouraged through classification and registration processes are clearly paying off in better conformation and better movement. On the other hand, it is of concern that certain basic principles of horsemanship are not as universal as they perhaps once were.

Part of the reason for this may be that fewer of us grow up around horses than used to be the case. Following the course of history from the agricultural and industrial eras to the current age of technology and information, horses in the western world are no longer predominantly farm animals, beasts of burden or war machines. Instead, they now occupy a predominantly recreational niche in an increasingly fast-paced world. Horses are regarded less as chattels or livestock and more as pets and partners in sport.

Like all revolutions, this change of status has both benefits and costs. Benefits come in the form of selective breeding and better health care, to give just two examples. Costs arise from a lack of familiarity with horses and their psychology.

Just like any game, sport or enterprise, the horse world has its rules, procedures and protocols. Learning what to do is a necessary process. The resulting skill brings greater confidence and is one of the building blocks of success. On the flip side, knowing what not to do, which is not always as simple as being the opposite of what to do, is also crucial.

Horses come in all types and sizes. On the outside they may look different, but on the inside their genetic make-up and physiology are essentially the same. All equines are grass-eating prey animals. Athletic, muscular and strong, their natural preference is to turn and flee from danger. If

CHAPTER 1: BEGINNINGS

attacked or cornered, however, they are capable of employing a range of very effective defence mechanisms with lightning speed and amazing force. They tend to shoot first and ask questions later.

Your horse is a purpose-built, finely tuned, beautifully balanced piece of natural engineering. He comes with a range of speeds, power steering, fantastic shock absorbers and leather upholstery. Like a car, your horse can go forwards, backwards, right and left. Your horse can also go sideways, up and down.

Unlike a car, which is metal, glass and rubber, your horse is a living, breathing being of flesh and blood. Your horse has emotions, moods and fears that are all his own. Furthermore, a car will not complain or feel cooped up if you leave it sitting in the garage for days, weeks or years. When you drive it out of the garage, it will not buck, snort or pigroot with the sheer joy of getting to stretch its legs – but a horse might. That's because horses are born to move of their own volition, whereas cars are made to be driven only when a driver turns the key. In the wild, the herd travels for most of the day and most of the night, from tuft of grass to tuft of grass, from the pasture to the water and back again. Now and then they will run, buck and play. Now and then they will doze or take a nap.

Thousands of years of evolution have made horses prone to stress and injuries resulting from unnatural physical and psychological demands. In view of this, it is actually something of a miracle that they take so kindly to stabling or being kept in a small yard, with hand-feeding replacing foraging, an artificial supply of water taking the place of trips to the stream, our company instead of the herd, and us dictating how much exercise they get and when.

Modern horse-keeping practices are a departure from what a horse considers natural, despite being what we humans consider desirable. To a horse, a lovely warm, dry stable of his own, with two or three carefully measured meals a day and an hour's exercise, can be hell on earth. He may feel trapped, vulnerable and alone; he cannot see whether predators are sneaking up; and he spends hours and hours with nothing to eat and nothing to do. All these things are bad for his mental health, digestive system and physical fitness. That's the bad news. The good news is that horses can adapt to living according to our convenience rather than to theirs, as long as the change is managed slowly and sympathetically and provided we cater for as many as their needs as possible.

Seven Steps to Success

Success with horses, irrespective of your goals, discipline or sport, hinges on seven simple steps.

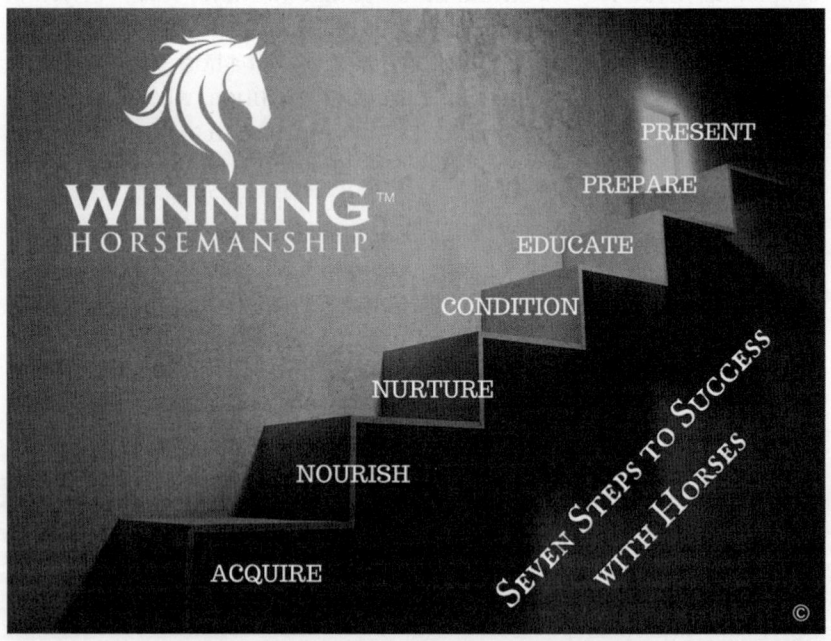

The Seven Steps to Success with Horses

CHAPTER 1: BEGINNINGS

They are:

Step 1. Acquire.

Step 2. Nourish.

Step 3. Nurture.

Step 4. Condition.

Step 5. Educate.

Step 6. Prepare.

Step 7. Present.

When you get these steps right, they will assist you and your horse to enjoy each other, help you to train your horse, improve your horse's holistic wellbeing and allow you to show your horse at its best.

They will also help you to reduce stress and enhance success across the board.

chapter 2

ACQUIRE

"Although it's rewarding to achieve recognition from others, the most treasured moments with your horse can't be measured by blue ribbons, awards, or levels earned. Those moments usually happen when you're alone with your horse because they're about the relationship, trust, understanding, lightness and connection you share together. They're about the partnership you've created."

ANNIE SHANK

chapter 2
Acquire

The Right Horse

Of all the horses I have owned and loved, I have only actually chosen one of them. To put it a different way, on one occasion I selected a horse I was interested in. I researched her breeding, had a test ride, bid for her at auction and took her home. That was Duell Star, nicknamed 'Duco', an athletic Hanoverian who became an eventer and later a broodmare.

Riding Duell Star in the cross-country phase at the Harden One Day Event, circa 1986. Photographer: Jack Pappas

Every other horse or pony was either chosen for me or chose me, inasmuch as they were gifts or I bred them or they were acquired on humane impulse.

CHAPTER 2: ACQUIRE

I am sharing this because it is often the same for others. We have acquired a horse, we love it and we want to do something with it. Unless all you want is an expensive and rather inefficient lawn mower, that something usually involves riding and sometimes competition.

Irrespective of your status or experience, the horse you have or the horse you want will have certain characteristics and aptitudes that will suit one discipline or activity over another. If these features coincide with your interests and ambitions, then there is perhaps a higher probability of success but definitely no guarantees. We all know stories where beautiful, high-priced, seemingly purpose-built horses have failed to triumph, counterbalanced by stories where horses that were too small, too old, or too difficult have succeeded against the odds.

> As a child I was inspired by the story of Stroller, the 14.1hh show jumping pony who took his young English rider, Marion Coakes, all the way to the Olympics. The partnership started in 1960, when Marion was about thirteen. At the end of Marion's junior career her father wanted to replace Stroller with a horse, but Marion wanted to keep riding Stroller. Nobody told Stroller that ponies couldn't out-jump horses and the pair won sixty-one open international competitions, along with an individual silver medal at the 1968 Olympics. In 1970, Stroller, still going strong at twenty years old, was named the leading show jumper at the Horse of the Year Show. Stroller was the only pony to compete in show jumping at the Olympics and the only pony to win the Hickstead Derby.
>
> Another true fairytale is that of Australia's Wendy Schaeffer and Sunburst. Sunburst and Wendy got together when he was a retired racehorse and she was eleven years old. Standing 15.3hh, Sunburst was bought as a Pony Club mount. When Wendy was seventeen, she was inspired by the gold medal success of the Australian Team at the 1992 Barcelona Olympics, so she set her sights on the Atlanta Olympics in 1996. Sunburst was not a big mover but his rideability saw him finish as the best of the Australian horses after the dressage phase in Atlanta.

> He followed that up with a clear cross-country round in the fourth fastest time and a clear round in the show jumping. In just ten years, Sunburst had gone from racehorse to Pony Club mount to top ranked international eventer to clinching back-to-back Olympic Team Gold for Australia with his twenty-one year old rider.

How far your horse can take you in any given sport or discipline depends on his aptitude and your ability to produce him at his best. Any sound horse can become fit enough to gallop 3,200 metres, but it takes special talent, not to mention a measure of luck, to win the Melbourne Cup.

How your horse is bred may be a clue to his potential. In general terms, we may think of Arabians as being suited to endurance riding; Quarter horses excelling in cutting, reining and western classes; Australian Stock Horses dominating in camp drafting and Warmbloods being purpose-bred for the Olympic sports. The saying 'horses for courses' didn't come out of nowhere!

As for all generalisations, however, there are exceptions and your horse may well be one of them. He may be an unlikely hero like Stroller or Sunburst, just waiting to be discovered.

The next step is to consider whether your horse's qualities and your own goals and aspirations are in alignment. This is not such a burning question if you simply want a pleasure horse for rides in the bush – it won't matter whether your horse is gold medal material or not, provided he is sane, safe and sure-footed. If your goals include the show ring or the competition arena, however, you will need to take into account what judges look for and assess your horse accordingly.

Unfortunately, especially at large shows with tight timetables, the opportunity for a judge to provide feedback to competitors is limited or non-existent, and dressage and other scoresheets do not allow for more than brief comments either.

CHAPTER 2: ACQUIRE

As a Warmblood Classifier evaluating suitability for breeding, one does have the luxury of only one exhibitor in the ring at a time. Classification is not about placing one horse by comparing it with several others. It is about scoring each animal on their individual merits to see whether they meet a predetermined standard for entry to a Stud Book. The process is similar in the case of an Assessment Tour, where an individual horse's score dictates its relative ranking on a national basis. It is also about seeing each animal at its best, ideally unrestricted by the athletic or technical skills of its handler. There is time for the classifiers to give that person individual feedback about their horse and suggestions on their own performance. When a horse is presented in a subsequent class and a recommended change has been made, it can be very rewarding to see the difference. That potential for improvement and how to get it is one of the reasons for writing this book.

Conformation seminar for the AWHA Ltd, Victoria, 2015.
Photographer: Mary McBurnie

Where there is an element of subjectivity, all good judges, classifiers and assessors seek to bring consistency to their job by carrying in their head an image of the ideal, perfect horse. They know that this imaginary creature does not exist, but they use it as a yardstick against which real horses are judged.

> **The challenge comes from what I think of as 'the judge's trade off'.**

It is more complicated than that, of course, because the judge's job is to make quick decisions about which horses in a given class come closest to the ideal. The challenge comes from what I think of as 'the judge's trade off'. To take a breed class for example, two or more horses may be of similar quality in terms of conformation, but one does not track up when it walks and the other paddles at the trot. Another does not move as well as its conformation would lead you to expect it should, whereas an entrant with inferior conformation moves very well. And so on. The judge must rank what they see in front of them on the day and do their best to be fair to all, as well as maintaining consistency from class to class, show to show, and year to year.

Let us examine the factors a judge takes into account.

Conformation

In subjective events like the show ring, and especially for the selection of breeding stock, conformation is very important. In objective events like show jumping, however, conformation is not assessed. Other events are judged on a combination of subjective and objective factors, which may be weighted differently by different judges. This is the reason why more than one judge is often employed and the scores are averaged.

Two key criteria apply to conformation. The first is that the horse should be correct, symmetrical and harmonious in terms of physics and levers. Such conformation predisposes the horse to a long and happy

CHAPTER 2: ACQUIRE

working life, as free as possible from strains placed on muscles, joints and ligaments by incorrect skeletal alignment. There are many good books on conformation, so we will not explore it in detail here but I do recommend that you study it and apply what you learn.

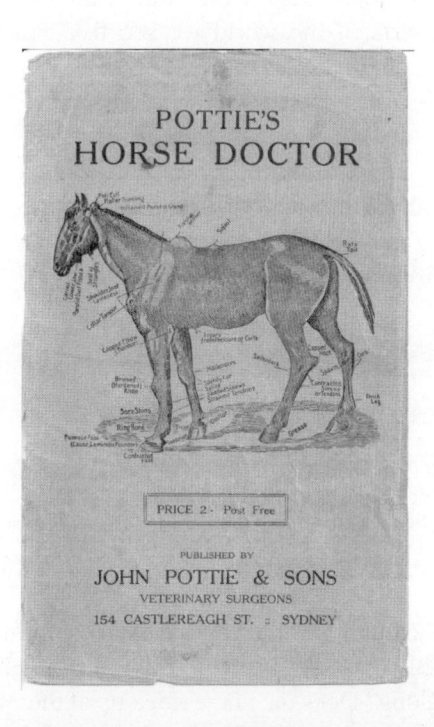

The cover of a wonderful old book, illustrating the characteristics you do NOT want your horse to have! Marchant & Co, Sydney 1954

The second criterion is that the horse's conformation, colour and overall build should be as close as possible to the ideal as set down by the relevant breed society. Breed Standards of Excellence encompass correct conformation but are also specific about desirable characteristics, like the dished face and high tail set of the Arabian, the musculature of a Quarter Horse, the feathers of the draught breeds or the colour of a Palomino.

Gaits

In Australia, most horses are assessed at three gaits, namely walk, trot and canter. The gallop is obviously very important in eventers and Thoroughbred racehorses, while some Standardbreds are natural pacers. In other parts of the world we see five-gaited saddle horses, native ponies that tölt, and a range of other gaits.

> My first pony, Beauty, performed a natural amble. It was incredibly comfortable and fun to ride, but I had to take care that she never broke into this gait when we were on show as it was most definitely frowned upon as incorrect, even at Pony Club.

Gaits need to be 'true', which means a four-beat walk, a two-beat trot and a three-beat canter with a period of suspension. When viewed from the front or behind, the legs should travel straight, they should not swing in or out and they certainly should not interfere with any of the other limbs. The horse should not show any lameness or unevenness.

Paces

'Paces' refers to the quality of the gaits. Is there rhythm and impulsion in all gaits? Does the horse look like he is going somewhere with purpose or just meandering along? Does the horse track up at the walk, which means that the hind feet at least step into the hoof prints of the forefeet? Are the hindquarters engaged, with the hind legs stepping well under the body? Does the canter show a clear 'jump' during the period of suspension? Do the paces appear elastic, athletic and ground covering? Is there a difference between collection and extension without loss of rhythm?

> *"One must think when looking at a horse in motion, that it hears music inside its head."*
>
> ANONYMOUS

CHAPTER 2: ACQUIRE

Rhythm is at the base of the dressage training scale, but it is by no means confined to dressage. Rhythm permeates everything horses do when they do it naturally. It should also permeate everything we do with them, from grooming to riding. Horses appreciate rhythm. As someone once observed, "One must think when looking at a horse in motion, that it hears music inside its head." The same principle can help us enormously. When you lead your horse, walk and run with rhythm; when you ride, ride with rhythm. Have a tune in your head and switch tunes when you change gaits. If you have the facilities to do so, play music while you work with your horse – have fun finding out his favourites and then use them to enhance your time together.

Focussing on rhythm can have the happy effect of taking your mind off a range of other things and your horsemanship will unconsciously improve as a result. A great exercise for improving both your feel and your appreciation of rhythm at the same time is to concentrate on your horse's inside hind leg. You can do this mounted or on the ground during lunging or liberty work. Watch/feel that leg and watch/feel what else moves when the inside hind foot leaves the ground. Count the beats – one, two, three, four at the walk, one–two at the trot, one–two–three at the canter. Which of your hips gets lifted with which hind foot? Which diagonal are you rising on at the trot? Which hind foot initiates the canter strike-off when leading with the near fore? At the gallop, just feel the four-beat rhythm for its own sake and enjoy its sheer power and glory.

Learning to See

> *"Educate your eye and then trust it!"*
>
> LYNNE CROWDEN

It isn't easy to be objective about your own horse. We look at them so often and know them so well that we can lose our ability to 'see' what they are really like. This tendency to bias is called stable blindness.

So, observe your horse from on the ground and, if he is started under saddle, from his back. What work seems to make him happiest? If he has competed, what classes has he won already? What feedback did you receive from the judge? The next step is to seek a second opinion (and ideally a third and fourth).

I am often asked how people can determine whether their colt is stallion material. My advice is to get a number of different opinions from knowledgeable equestrians. They do not need to be completely independent, just sufficiently impartial to be able to put aside any bias towards or against your horse and his bloodlines, and sufficiently experienced to be able to see a horse's true conformation and way of going without being dazzled by the presence and gloss of a colt.

Whatever you have in mind for your horse, if you have asked someone for their opinion, make sure you listen carefully and courteously. They may be wrong, they may be right, but they have done you a favour by sharing their observations. The truth about your horse will probably be somewhere between the most enthusiastic and most critical reviews, hence the desirability of showing him to a range of people. If distance is an issue, you can always send a video for comment.

Test your own 'eye' too. How do the comments of your review panel compare to your own thoughts about your horse's strengths and weaknesses?

One tip I received years ago was to pretend that your horse belongs to your worst enemy! Look at him carefully (your horse, not your enemy) with a view to finding every fault. Be very, very picky. Does that change the way he looks to you? If you already have a good eye, it shouldn't make much difference. And the more horses you evaluate, the better your eye will get. Take the opportunity to practise when you are out and about. Pay particular attention at breed shows and see if you would have handed out the ribbons in the same order as the judge. If not, try to find out why.

Once you are armed with a good idea of your horse's likely career path, you can begin to enhance his natural qualities even further. Horses are immensely adaptable, but there are limits to how comfortably a square peg can occupy a round hole, so work to his – and your – strengths as far as possible.

A different dilemma faces the average owner of an exceptional horse who feels the need 'to let him prove himself'. It is not unheard of for people to go into debt paying trainers and riders in order to further their horse's career 'because he deserves a chance'. If you are a breeder and the fame and glory will bring more customers to your stud, then maybe it is a reasonable and rational economic decision. But my advice would be not to do it for the horse's sake alone. Believe me, your horse will be perfectly happy to eat, play and sleep in a nice paddock. Thoughts of gold medals and flowery garlands will never once cross his mind, nor will he ever wish he was in a truck, ferry or cargo plane, bound for an important event.

The Right Gear

Before you even bring a new horse home, you will need some basic equipment. These include utensils, like a water container, feed bin and hay net; a halter and lead rope; grooming gear; and tools like a cleaning kit for your saddlery, along with a shovel, rake and manure receptacle.

If you want to do a lot of riding you will also want a saddle and saddle cloth for your horse to wear, along with proper boots and a safety helmet for yourself. Depending on the climate and where you keep your horse, you might want to add horse rugs of the appropriate weight to keep him clean, warm and dry, or to prevent his coat from getting bleached by the sun.

If you want to compete, you will need to buy, borrow or hire a few extra items:

- A safe horse truck or horse float plus a vehicle capable of towing it.
- Float boots, tail bag, tail bandages etc.
- Rugs and hoods or neck rugs for home and for show day. Make sure all clothing fits comfortably, including when the horse's head is down.

- Depending on the show and the classes you are entering, you will want a show halter and lead and/or show bridle and saddle.

- Shampoo, conditioner, etc.

- Show attire for yourself.

Some of the above will require a substantial investment, so plan your purchases and budget accordingly.

There can be subtle stylistic differences between classes, so opt for equipment that will be as versatile as possible and build on it from there. You may also be able to accessorise to a degree. Rhinestones, which used to be the exclusive province of Hollywood cowboys, have now been enthusiastically embraced by the English riding world.

TIP ▶ A plain leather bridle will take you anywhere, but if you hanker for bling in events that allow it, then by all means purchase a flamboyant brow band. Make sure its size and shape flatters your horse's head and it is adjusted for his comfort.

TIP ▶ If you compete in Western events, you can start with good-quality leather equipment and add silver to your saddlery piece by piece.

Katie Umback has competed in Pony Club, dressage, eventing, hacking, show jumping and equitation. Katie is now an international dressage competitor and an experienced dressage and hack judge. I have enormous respect for Katie and her achievements, not least because she has learned to ride twice! The second time around involved a very different body, one that had survived serious neck, spinal and pelvic injuries sustained as a younger rider, only to be ravaged by progressive multiple sclerosis (MS) which incapacitated her for six long years and threatened to confine her to a wheelchair for life. Katie clung to her dreams, new medication brought some improvement and she has now adapted to riding with her 'MS body', despite seventy percent numbness, chronic pain, cramping, fatigue and diminished strength.

CHAPTER 2: ACQUIRE

In her thirty-eight years in the equestrian industry, Katie has seen a few changes and predicts a few more.

"When I first started showing, we used to use open-nosed bridles with nonosebands, plain leather brow bands and everyone rode in an all-purpose saddle. Show saddles were not invented then and dressage and jumping saddles were very rare and expensive. Our show attire was very plain and show jackets didn't come in an array of colours back then. Usually they were navy or chocolate brown in colour, with a long-sleeved cotton shirt, tie, crochet gloves and velvet caps with chin straps. Later on, riding jackets were predominantly black, with very long tails that covered the saddle and white stocks and bowler hats.

As time went by, riding jackets started to come in different colours, then in different patterns and we started wearing vests under our jackets. In the past eight to ten years, coloured stocks started replacing ties. Our show attire became more colourful and our jackets got much shorter in length; plaited brow bands also started matching our attire. In the past couple of years, bling started to appear in our brow bands, on top of our hacking canes, in lapels, on our jackets and now people are 'blinging' out their attire and equipment wherever they can. I can just see it getting more fancy, sparkly and complicated in time.

In the dressage ring I can see the bling thing growing more and more as well. Once upon a time the dressage was very formal with plain equipment and we all looked like butlers but now, bling has started to leach out into our brow bands, on our stirrup irons, spurs, trimmings on our jackets, breeches, stocks and helmets. Our jackets and stocks are not so formal looking, with people starting to use colour more, so I can see dressage attire becoming more show-like."

If your everyday bridle and saddle are of reasonable quality, well-fitting and clean, they will do perfectly well for events where the equipment and turnout of the horse are not critical to success. This would include dressage, show jumping, eventing, reining, cutting, camp drafting and polo. If you are entering the Garryowen, on the other hand, where presentation and correctness are very important, pretty much everything you and your horse wear in the ring will be heavily influenced by tradition with an emphasis on quality.

It is possible to ride without a bridle or a saddle and many of us did so as children, but for most people this is the end game, not the beginning. It is not necessarily practical or safe for the average rider; nor is it likely to meet the rules and requirements of many organisations and sports.

TIP ▶ Learn the rules and know what is required.

TIP ▶ If you keep your equipment inventory up to date and include receipts and photographs of items, it will be handy if you ever need to make an insurance claim.

chapter 3

Animal magnetism!
Photographer: Jack Pappas

NOURISH

"Good Luck is rather particular who she rides with, and mostly prefers those who have got common sense and a good heart; at least that is my experience."

ANNA SEWELL, 'BLACK BEAUTY'

chapter 3

NOURISH

The benefits of optimal nutrition, in terms of winning horsemanship, are that horses fed a balanced ration of macro- and micro-nutrients, just like elite human athletes who nourish their bodies as a priority, will be able to work harder for longer, will have better immunity, sustain fewer injuries and, if they do become ill or injured, will recover faster. And, just like children who receive optimal nutrition, your horse will be calmer and have a longer attention span.

Every body – horse or human – needs the right balance of exercise, recovery and nutrition. To look his best and do his best, your horse needs top notch nutrition. So do you. Often, horses and people don't do well because they don't feel well. Nutrition is the foundation of holistic wellbeing. If we give the body what it needs, it can work wonders, including reversing disease and restoring health.

Horses need good-quality feed, free from mould, dust and other contaminants. Our aim is to provide a balanced ration of macronutrients, incorporating protein, carbohydrates and fats in the right ratio, along with a synergistic combination of micronutrients, incorporating vitamins, minerals, trace elements and antioxidants.

Long-term deficiencies of nutrients in the body (an unbalanced diet), combined with a build-up of toxins (like air pollution, pesticides, herbicides, drugs, poisonous plants, mould and fungus) can lead to degenerative diseases such as arthritis, cancer, auto-immune problems, organ failure, allergies, and lowered immunity to parasites and infection. In humans, we know that as high as 80 percent of chronic conditions can be prevented by better lifestyle choices. The same is true for horses and it is up to us to make those choices on their behalf.

Not only are the contents of the ration important, the feeding schedule itself is also a key element to success. When we get this right, the outcomes include optimal digestion, healthy weight, elastic skin, shiny hair, strong hooves, good muscle tone, a strong resilient skeleton, enhanced immunity, better recovery and improved mood. When we get it wrong, over time nutritional imbalances will wreak havoc on your horse's body. In the shorter term, poor feeding practices can lead to teeth problems and/or digestive upsets, like colic and ulcers, with consequences including pain, suffering and even the death of the horse, not to mention missed training and missed competitions on your part.

What Horses Want

> *What horses want can be summed up in two four-letter words. Those words are 'herd' and 'herb'.*
>
> JOANNE VERIKIOS

As we know, horses are herd animals, meaning they feel most comfortable in a group of other horses; and they are herbivores, meaning all their nutritional needs are supposed to be met by the plants they eat, as dictated by the soil in which those plants grow. Specifically, horses evolved to graze on long-stem fibrous plants like grass.

In the wild, horses also browse on branches, twigs and leaves, rather like short-necked giraffes. All these bits and pieces provide different nutrients, so it is little wonder that our domesticated horses occasionally ring-bark the tastier trees in their paddocks or chew on our wooden fences and stable doors.

Do not underestimate the value of turnout time with some green pick. Benefits include:

- Exercise.
- Fresh air and enjoyment of open space.
- Relaxation and stress relief.
- Stretching, especially along the top line.

- Nasal drainage.

- Massage, through the contact of the hooves with the earth and through rolling on the ground or rubbing on trees and posts.

- Using teeth and jaws the way nature intended, which is beneficial for oral and dental health.

- The opportunity to interact with other horses, including mutual grooming.

- Access to grass, their natural food.

- Entertainment, because grazing keeps them busy and the outlook provides variety.

> *To a horse, turnout in a paddock with grass is the equivalent of us going to a health retreat.*
>
> JOANNE VERIKIOS

My father's pharmacy had a view of one of the paddocks where I used to keep my ponies.

The ponies were predominantly grass fed, but I used to give them a small ration of chaff and bran in the morning when I looked them over before school and in the evening after I had been riding.

Their favourite food, however, was supplied by my mother who would keep a bucket handy in the kitchen for fruit and vegetable peelings, the outer leaves of lettuce, pumpkin seeds and so on. The ponies absolutely relished this with their breakfast and their coats bloomed from all the extra antioxidants and minerals they were getting. They ate pretty much everything that was in the bucket, except for onion skins and citrus peel.

CHAPTER 3: NOURISH

> One day, one of Dad's racehorse trainer customers came to the dispensary door and said, "My word Trevor, those ponies look well. What's your secret?" "Scraps," said Dad. "Scraps!" the man echoed, "Pull the other one!" I think he thought my father had some miracle tonic and was holding out on him.

For some equines, good pasture or good quality hay will supply all their energy needs. The only reasons for hand-feeding beyond hay are to compensate for deficiencies or nutritional imbalances in the pasture or if the animal has particular nutritional requirements that can only be met by supplementary feeding.

Note that when we talk about 'good' pasture, we mean that there is enough acreage per horse (seven acres or three hectares per horse is an old rule of thumb), the pasture contains mixed grasses, there are few weeds and no poisonous ones, the grass has not recently been sprayed with toxic chemicals, and manure is removed regularly.

Matching the horse's needs for energy with the amount of exercise he is receiving is an art – one which it will pay dividends to learn because it will make your horse happier, healthier and far more manageable from foal to weanling, weanling to young horse, young to mature horse and mature to aged horse.

It is most important to recognise and adjust for stages of growth and for the needs of horses doing different jobs. A pregnant mare will have different nutritional requirements from a lightly-worked gelding. A young stallion in his first couple of seasons at stud is likely to expend a great deal more nervous energy than a well-seasoned sire. Horses shown in led classes don't do much work beyond basic conditioning and so do not require as much energy in their food as performance horses doing hard physical work such as race horses, eventers, endurance horses or stock horses.

As a general observation, far too many horses are overfed and underworked, which is bad for their physical and mental health; not to mention their owner's safety and wallets.

The bulk of a horse's food intake should come from roughage in the form of long-stem fibre, i.e., grass or hay. They need to chew, they need plenty of bulk to keep their digestive system happy and they need to eat little and often. Picking at grass or hay throughout the day and night meets this need. The horse has a single stomach and a small digestive tract which does not cope well with large, infrequent meals.

TIP ▶ The more grass they get, the less hay they will need; the less grass they get, the more hay they will need.

Is chaff the same as hay? Yes and no. Is chaff a substitute for grass or hay? Definitely not! Technically, there is no difference between the two because chaff is simply chopped hay. In terms of benefit to your horse, however, hay is king. Because the chaff cutter has already done a reasonable job of beginning the chewing process, chaff can cause teeth and digestive problems. Chewing is good for a horse's teeth and oral health; the more chewing he does, the better his teeth will wear and the happier and healthier he will be. Eating too much chaff means that the teeth don't wear as they should, so the horse will need to see his dentist more often.

The nature of chaff also allows the horse to eat his complete ration too fast and then have nothing to nibble on for the rest of the day or night. It is simply not natural for his system to have a lot of food to process in one go and then very little for hours.

TIP ▶ As a guide, feed only enough chaff to stop a horse from bolting his hard feed, with the rest of the ration being fed as hay.

TIP ▶ Two or three small feeds daily are better (and safer) for your horse's digestion than one big meal. As a guideline, provide, say, a quarter of the concentrate ration in the morning, a quarter at midday, and the other half at night, along with *ad lib* hay or grass.

CHAPTER 3: NOURISH

TIP ▶ The amount of grain or other concentrates (such as pre-mixes and pelleted rations) will depend on the horse's size and condition. It should vary according to the individual horse's workload and be measured by weight of the feed in proportion to the horse's bodyweight.

TIP ▶ Add or increase hard feed very conservatively, monitor the results (including your horse's behaviour in different environments) and then adjust as required. Remember that the role of hard feed is as a supplement to grass or hay, not as a replacement for it.

High-quality, science-based commercial mixes can be useful as an alternative to grain. Their main advantages are to simplify feeding and they can be more economical and practical than buying and storing all of the individual components. Do read the label, however, and be honest and sensible about what your horse needs. 'Super-Racehorse-Magic-Formula' may sound sexy but feeding it to your horse when your goal is a relaxing weekend trail ride will not do either of you any favours!

Members of the Cumburrie Trail Riding Club taking a break during a ride in 1977. Peter Williams on the left, R.M. Williams second from the right and Leanne Jones standing with my grey pony, Cloud. Photographer: Joanne Verikios

Energy to Burn

Finessing the energy component of a horse's ration seems to present the greatest challenge to the average horse owner. If a horse receives too much energy-producing feed without enough regular exercise to burn it off, he becomes overexcited very easily. This may not be obvious at home, where he may behave quite well during his regular routine. In a new environment, however, with stimulating sights and sounds, the promise of more space to explore and new horses to mix with, our normally placid horse may 'feel his oats' and play up.

A quick examination of the composition of feeds commonly given to horses, based on a simple starch scale equivalent, will show how easy it is to over feed energy-producing ingredients.

Lucerne hay or chaff comprises about 45 percent energy and 15 percent protein. As such, lucerne is an excellent choice as the basis of a ration, supplying an alternative to good pasture which has about the same values. Oaten or wheaten hay and chaff, on the other hand, offer around 35 percent energy, 6 percent protein and are low in calcium, with a poor calcium to phosphorous ratio, so should only be fed in small amounts. Bran and pollard both contain around 40 percent energy and 10 percent protein. Bran has a role to play as a source of low-energy bulk in a ration, so up to 1½ to 2 kilograms can be divided amongst a day's feeds. On the other hand, pollard is not a good choice for horses because it can swell in the gut, causing colic. Pollard has also been associated with bacterial toxins.

Moving from roughage to concentrates, we discover that grains are much higher in energy, with oats at 60 percent, barley at 70 percent, and corn or maize coming in at 80 percent.

> **TIP ▶** Horses in light work simply do not require this level of energy – if you are going to feed grain it means you must exercise and work your horse hard or it will virtually be jumping out of its skin.

CHAPTER 3: NOURISH

Oats have 10 percent protein along with a fairly high fibre content. Oats may be fed whole, but crushed or rolled oats are often preferred to help to avoid digestive problems. Barley is usually fed crushed, soaked or boiled. Corn is preferably fed cracked because its outer coating is rather indigestible. Cracking corn, however, leads to rapid oxidation, so it should ideally be consumed within two weeks or nutrients will be lost. Because corn is very high in energy and heavier in terms of weight per volume than oats, it should be measured with care and fed sparingly.

The old timers used to like to feed a bit of corn to enrich the coat of show horses, because it was thought to 'heat the blood'. That's one way of describing the effect it can have, especially if used to excess. A little goes a long way.

> Mr Watterson fed and exercised all the race horses in his care as individuals, and as appropriate to their age, constitution, temperament and level of training. The same went for his lead pony, Star, whose job it was to be ridden to the racetrack and back (this was well before horse trailers were commonplace) while Mr Watterson ponied two racehorses, leading one on each side.
>
> Star's role was to be a steady influence on these young, ultra-fit and highly strung Thoroughbreds. In other words, grain was not on Star's menu.
>
> One day, Mr Watterson noticed that Star was a bit excitable. The next day Star was getting even friskier and by the third day he was cavorting like a racehorse.
>
> Mr Watterson knew that Star's feed ration wasn't the problem. It was a mystery – until he noticed his wife feeding the chickens in the back yard and then giving Star something as well. "What did you give the pony?" he asked her. "Just half a handful of the chooks' corn. Why?" she replied.

Oil-based feeds can be useful to improve the texture and shine of the coat, but be aware that they are very high in energy too. Sunflower meal, for example, contains roughly 36 percent protein and 45 percent energy. Its residual oil converts to an extra 8 percent energy, making sunflower meal similar to oats in energy terms. Cotton seed meal is even more energy dense than corn.

TIP ▶ The moral of the story is to treat grain, concentrates and oil-based feeds as additives rather than staples and plan your ration with care to avoid the danger of excess energy.

TIP ▶ Always make dietary changes gradually – say over a week at least. A 'change' includes coming in from grass to the stable, or switching from one mix to another.

> *If your ration changes are not incremental, the outcome may be excremental!*
>
> JOANNE VERIKIOS

Gradual changes let you monitor your horse's reaction to the new feed. Is it making him hotter or calmer? Does he clean it all up with gusto or does he pick through it and leave some food uneaten in his feed bin? The ration must also be economical, as simple as possible and palatable to the horse. It must provide the right balance of energy, protein, minerals and vitamins.

TIP ▶ Always mix feeds as you need them, not in advance, so they are as fresh as possible at each feed time. Always dispose of any leftovers from the previous meal.

A horse's feed needs are calculated by bodyweight. Step one is to establish what your horse weighs. You can do this with scales if available or with a girth weight tape. Step two is to work out the weight of each element of your horse's ration (hay, grain, chaff, bran, proprietary mix, etc.). Step three is to choose buckets, scoops and measures that will help you to repeat the same proportions reliably. Step four is to weigh the feed per container to get the ration right.

CHAPTER 3: NOURISH

TIP ▶ As a very rough guide, a horse requires 2 kilograms of dry matter daily per 100 kilograms of bodyweight. So a 500 kilogram horse (around 15–16hh) requires about 10 kilograms of feed, of which the bulk must be fibrous for good gut function. For example, 60 to 70 percent could be hay and chaff, another 15 percent could be bran and the rest made up of grain, concentrates and oil seed meals.

TIP ▶ Be aware that the weight of hay can vary from batch to batch, so once you know the weight of hay your horse needs (e.g., 1 or 2 percent of his bodyweight daily), you can feed a larger or smaller portion of a bale accordingly.

Always observe, remember, compare. Watch your horse and adjust his ration and workload as required. Monitor his condition closely, so that he does not get too fat or too thin. You should be able to feel his ribs but not see them.

Especially do not let foals, weanlings, yearlings and other immature horses get too fat and heavy, as this can be detrimental to their growth plates. We want our horses to last a long time, so it is better to keep your youngsters in healthy, lean condition than to overfeed them and have them suffer joint problems later.

> *"A true horseman does not look at the horse with his eyes; he looks at his horse with his heart."*
>
> ANONYMOUS

Let your horse finish his hard feed and preferably have an hour or so to start digesting it before you work him. The harder he is to work, the more time you should allow so that his circulatory system is available to pump oxygen to his muscles, rather than servicing his digestive needs. At the end of the workout, cool your horse off properly and let his heart and lungs return to their resting state before offering another meal.

On the other hand, you don't want to work a horse on a completely empty stomach. In nature, a horse's digestive tract always has something going through it, so an empty stomach is unnatural and stressful. Furthermore, vigorous exercise can cause stomach acid to splash upwards, leading to a form of heartburn and even ulcers.

TIP ▶ Feed a small portion of chaff, hay or grass before your workout if it has been more than two hours since the horse last ate.

Prevention is better than cure and these simple, common sense precautions are better than dealing with a case of colic, muscle spasms or founder.

Horses are creatures of habit and definitely appreciate being fed according to a predictable schedule. That said, to prepare your horse for those inevitable days when routine cannot be maintained, it is worth allowing slight variations to the schedule now and then.

> My stallion, Highborn Powerlifter, had a unique response when his breakfast was late.
>
> Power spent most of the day in a twenty acre paddock with hills, trees, a dam and a million dollar view, but he was often stabled at night. His dinner was served in a feed bin on the stable door, with a big rubber tub on the floor for hay.
>
> If I slept in beyond the time he was usually fed breakfast, Power would begin his protest routine by rattling the feed bin against the door, starting gently at first and then, using a variety of creative drumming rhythms, working up to a crescendo. Sometimes I even went back to sleep after the finale because the feed bin had come off the door and all was quiet again.
>
> By the time I got down to the stables I would find that he had passed the time by neatly stacking all of his containers according to size like Russian dolls. The feed bin would be inside the water bucket, which was inside the hay tub, always next to the wall to the right of the door!

Feeding to Win

We have already explored the basics of what to feed, when and why. Let us now turn to some 'secret' ingredients that will make your horse bloom and help him to stay sound and healthy for a long working life.

First, a little science lesson. Scientists are increasingly identifying links between the gut and the brain, between body movement and gut movement, and between gut health and mental health. This has long been acknowledged in humans, with 'having a gut reaction' or 'listening to your gut' being common phrases. What is being referred to are instinct and intuition – or elements of our superconscious intelligence.

Research is now showing many other fascinating interrelationships between the digestive, endocrine and neurological systems including:

- The role of the gut and gut bacteria in maintaining a healthy immune system.

- A high correlation between certain types of brain and intestinal disorders, including findings that, in humans at least, the brain–gut balance has an antidepressant role.

As one mammalian cell is very similar to another in structure, I will not be surprised if further studies reliably extrapolate these relationships to horses. In the meantime, this topic is important, because the optimal interplay between cells – the building blocks of life – is critically influenced by nutrition.

In the sections above we have discussed the macronutrients that make up the bulk of a horse's diet. In an ideal world, the macronutrients would also contain all the necessary micronutrients, more commonly known as vitamins and antioxidants, minerals and trace elements; just as they did when the earth was younger. Even where soils once contained more minerals, modern farming methods, including broad-acre harvesting and the extensive use of artificial fertilisers, herbicides and pesticides, have led to serious soil depletion over the years.

In turn, this leads to deficiencies and imbalances in the animals that eat plants, including horses and humans. Furthermore, grasses vary from region to region, soil to soil and they too have differing nutritional values from species to species. Some weeds are poisonous to horses, especially in drought conditions where there is little choice of pasture and the horses will eat things they would ordinarily avoid. For example, eating the weed known both as Patterson's Curse or Salvation Jane over a protracted period can cause cumulative liver damage. Phytotoxins and mycotoxins can proliferate during certain seasonal conditions and have been linked to mares miscarrying their foals.

Supplementation

> *...unless micronutrients are topped up before they are used up, we and our horses age faster.*

Do horses need nutritional supplements and if so, what kind? Let's borrow an analogy from physician and nutrition expert, Dr Alberto Peña Del Moral. Think of your horse (and yourself for that matter) as being like a photocopier, which comes complete with a set of toners. You provide it with a power source and some paper. Let's call these its macronutrients. Fed on paper and electricity, our machine will reliably produce copy after copy. Over time, however, the copies will get fainter and fainter until the machine stops working altogether. Why? Because it runs low on toner. Unless all the colours are present at the moment the copier needs to draw on them, it will send an error message until they are replaced. Toner for a photocopier is like micronutrients for an animal and copies of copies are similar to damaged cells. There is a limit on the number of times damaged cells can be reproduced, so unless micronutrients are topped up before they are used up, we and our horses age faster.

An animal has no 'low toner' warning light to indicate when it will require extra micronutrients, and individual needs change every fraction of a second. Some nutrients can be manufactured by the body but other

CHAPTER 3: NOURISH

essential nutrients must be constantly available to keep our reserves topped up. For instance, the body cannot make zinc or copper, so it has to obtain these minerals through food.

The body does eventually send us messages that different nutrients are in imbalance or low supply, usually in the form of disease symptoms. For example, animals with low levels of copper may exhibit a washed-out looking coat colour or a symptom known as 'spectacles' with rings around their eyes. The answer, however, does not simply lie in adding more of a single ingredient. The biochemical relationships in the body are far more complex and subtle than that, and a holistic approach is required to avoid imbalances. Healthy cells mean healthy tissues which make up a healthy body.

TIP ▶ It follows, then, that the best time to have these compounds available is all the time, which means they need to be in the grass and/or the feed ration.

Many commercial feed mixes and mineral salt blocks are fortified with additional vitamins and minerals. However, be aware that you may not be able to feed your horse enough of the mix to satisfy his daily micronutrient needs without blowing his mind with too much energy. Furthermore, his use of a salt lick is likely to be governed by his taste for salt, making that an unreliable source also.

I recommend the daily use of a high-quality, comprehensive equine multivitamin and mineral supplement. There are some good vitamin/mineral supplements available for horses, but as with the products manufactured for humans, quality can vary. Do some research and find a supplement manufacturer you can trust. Provided the formula you choose is comprehensive, balanced and does not contain any ingredients that can be toxic in excess, the horse's body will gratefully metabolise what it needs and harmlessly excrete the rest, just as nature intended. Consult your equine veterinarian for specific advice.

TIP ▶ The best way to give supplements to your horse is mixed into the feed. Dampening the ration will prevent your horse from sifting powdered supplements to the bottom of the feed bin.

TIP ▶ Electrolytes are a valuable addition for hard-working performance horses because they help to replace body salts that are excreted with sweat.

TIP ▶ Electrolytes can also have a positive effect on young, nervous horses. Feeding an electrolyte supplement before and after travel, thereby replacing body salts, can lead to a calmer horse.

TIP ▶ If you are not feeding an oil-based meal, then adding from a couple of tablespoons to half a cup of vegetable or coconut oil to your horse's feed ration will enrich the texture of his coat and provide essential fatty acids.

chapter 4

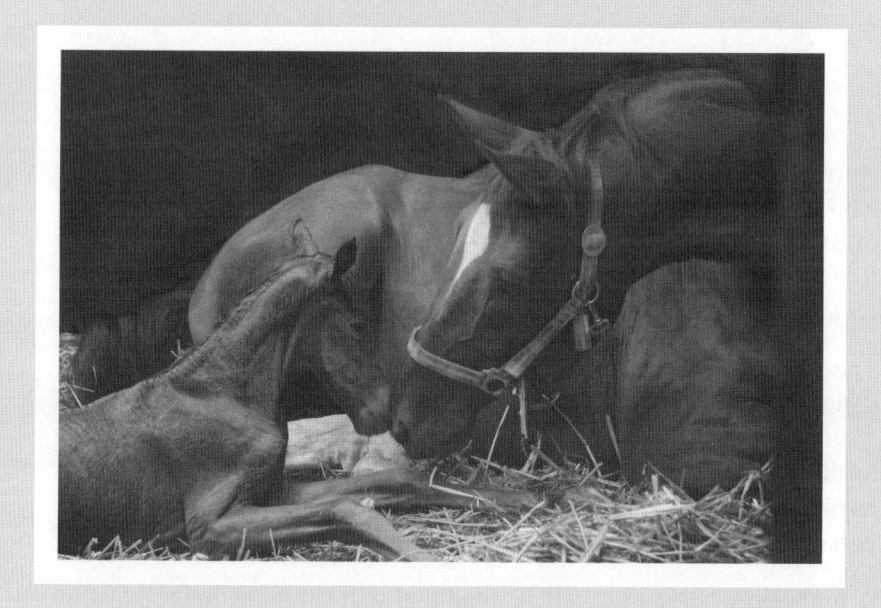

Nurture

"A great horseman or horsewoman has the curiosity of a foal, the patience of a mare and the drive of a stallion."

Joanne Verikios

chapter 4
Nurture

The Horse

Nurture as a verb means 'to care for and protect (someone or something) while they are growing, i.e., to bring up, care for, provide for, take care of, attend to, look after, rear, support, raise, foster, parent, mother, tend'. It is also used to mean 'to feed, to nourish', which we have already covered in the previous chapter.

The word 'nurture', therefore, is all about horsemanship, because domesticated horses are dependent upon their owners to replace what Mother Nature would normally provide for them in the wild. It relates to those aspects of husbandry and management that keep our horses happy and healthy, sane and sound, willing and winning in your chosen pursuit.

A fit, healthy horse in excellent condition will catch the judge's eye in led, breed and hack classes and will be able to acquit himself well in other ridden events. A fit, healthy horse will look forward to his training sessions and his outings, whereas a horse that is off-colour for whatever reason will not. A fit, healthy horse will be fertile, and well-equipped to sire or carry a healthy foal.

Hydration

Part of your job is to ensure that your horse always has access to more water than he needs, so there is no risk of him going short. Why? There are two main reasons: digestion and heat control. Horses need plenty of clean, fresh water available twenty-four hours a day, seven days a week, every day of the year. A lot of water is required to help keep all that roughage moving through the digestive system. Impaction colic is a life-threatening problem when the digestive system gets blocked and will need immediate veterinary attention.

CHAPTER 4: NURTURE

Water is also necessary to make up for what is lost in breathing, sweating and urination. A thirsty horse should always be allowed to drink or he will become dehydrated. Even after vigorous work, he should be offered a few good swallows of tepid water, then be walked to cool off a bit, then offered more and so on until he has drunk his fill and his heart rate and breathing have returned to normal. As with human marathon runners, horses taking part in endurance events or long trail rides should be allowed to drink along the way.

Actual water consumption varies according to the size of the horse, the heat of the day, how the horse is kept and how hard the horse works or sweats. A 15–16hh horse may drink 30 to 50 litres per day, with up to 70 litres of water a day being normal for a larger horse. A mare with a foal at foot needs plenty of water to make milk. Horses eating a dry ration will drink more than horses on grass with a high water content. Give them more than they need and keep it clean and fresh.

Probably because of their excellent sense of smell, horses will usually refuse to drink polluted or stagnant water. A challenge for competitors who travel to events is that their horses may also reject perfectly good water that is simply different from what they are used to. Strategies for dealing with this include the following:

- Take containers of water from home to provide familiar water for the day.

- If your horse is accustomed to drinking from a dam, take a scoop of mud with you in a plastic container and drop a bit into a bucket of unfamiliar water.

- Flavour the water at home with a little molasses for a few days beforehand and then add molasses to the new water until the horse has accepted it.

Always keep an eye on newly arrived horses to make sure that they are drinking enough after you bring them home. Dehydration can occur quickly, particularly in hot weather or if the horse has developed nervous diarrhoea from the stress of the trip or the thrill of meeting new friends.

TIP ▶ If they are eating but not drinking, then serve their hay and feed ration liberally moistened with water (and molasses if required).

You may also have to show a horse how to use an automatic drinker in a new stable. Fortunately most horses pick this skill up very quickly, but be prepared to put a water bucket in the corner if yours doesn't.

Dental Care

Check your horse's teeth regularly by following a simple one, two, three routine:

1. Watch your horse eat. If food or drool drops out of his mouth as he chews, he may have a sharp edge on a tooth that needs attention. Make a habit of looking around the feed bin after meals. Has he been dropping food?

2. Gently run your hands up the outside of his jaw, feeling along the tooth line, first on the left, then on the right. Does your horse flinch or can you feel any sharp edges through the skin of his face?

3. Open your horse's lips now and then and inspect his front teeth and gums. Is there any sign of uneven wear or gum disease? Are there any grass seeds stuck in his teeth and gums?

TIP ▶ The above routine will also help accustom him to having his mouth handled, which will make life easier when dentists, vets and judges wish to inspect it.

Even if you don't detect any problems, it is a good idea to get an equine veterinarian or qualified equine dentist to give your horse a regular oral check-up. If your horse is stabled and/or eating a lot of hard feed, then the intervals should be shorter. Youngsters between two and six years old should have their teeth checked every six months. Professional inspection and rasping of teeth is often necessary to prevent or alleviate pain, resistance, gum disease, digestive and even riding problems. Is he harder to bridle than he used to be? Has he started pulling, lugging more to one side or the other, or getting behind the bit? Does he shake his head or hold it more to one side or the other? Does he have a pained expression on his face? A visit from the dentist or chiropractor may work wonders.

First visit from the dentist. Photographer: Jack Pappas

TIP▶ If the dentist has had a bit of work to do, give the horse a day or two to recover before working him in a bridle again.

TIP▶ Before starting or mouthing young horses, ensure that an equine dentist has checked their teeth.

Feeding Positions

As often as possible, we should allow the horse to eat as nature intended, which means reaching his lips all the way down to the ground. I realise feeding your horse at ground level is not possible with hay nets tied to floats and trucks when you are out and about, because the net needs to be high enough so there is no danger of the horse getting tangled in it, even when it is empty. It may also not be practical in the case of some horses who overturn their feed bins and throw feed around (although a couple of large, smooth stones or a heavy salt lick will slow them down and may cause them to develop new habits over time).

However, the teeth align best and wear most evenly when eating long stem forage with the head and neck extended downwards. Other benefits include active stretching and stress release. Having the head down is a calm position for horses. Having the head up is an alert position and having it held very high is a stressed and hyper-vigilant posture. Stables and feed bins may replace what nature provides, but they can never improve on it.

Horse dentists recommend that you feed your horse where he has 360 degrees of vision – again as nature intended. Otherwise, his tendency as a prey animal is to try to glance around while eating, often with the unfortunate result of chewing more on one side than the other. This one-sided eating tendency causes the teeth to wear on a slant, which has consequences for the way the horse goes under saddle and will probably result in constant oral pain as well.

If you use a hanging feed bin, the best place for it is on a fence or gate, no higher than chest level, with good all-round visibility. A horse who looks like a chess knight when he is eating is not a comfortable horse. The second best place is on a stable door so the horse can see out. The worst place is in the corner of a stable or against a solid wall, where visibility is limited. In such cases, it might be better to close the door at meal times, so the horse is less inclined to look around and can concentrate on eating his feed.

> *When you're a horseman, you have to learn to think like a horse, not like a human. Just because you prefer to eat off a plate on a table doesn't mean your horse wouldn't prefer to eat off the ground.*
>
> JOANNE VERIKIOS

My advice is to mimic nature as far as possible, most of the time. Then the occasional compromise when you can't control the environment won't matter so much.

CHAPTER 4: NURTURE

It is also up to you to use natural and creative ways to look after your horse's mental needs by replacing what his environment may be missing in terms of companionship and mental stimulation. That can be as simple as spending time grooming or just sitting around with your horse, turning him out in a paddock, providing a companion animal or providing boredom busters like horse balls and other toys.

Listening to Your Horse

Your horse cannot talk, but when you learn to listen with all your senses, if you are lucky he will tell you that something is wrong so that you can make the necessary changes to help him. I say "if you are lucky" because some horses are very stoic and may not communicate their discomfort. Others let you know in no uncertain terms.

Lameness is usually fairly obvious – you can see or hear it when the horse is led (but only if you look and listen) and feel and hear it when the horse is ridden (but only if you have sensitive hands and seat and a listening ear). The art is then in determining which leg is lame, and what part of the limb is the seat of the problem.

Less obvious signals may include your horse beginning to resent being bridled, saddled, girthed up or mounted, when he wasn't like that before. He may suddenly become 'ticklish' in certain areas when being brushed. His facial expression may change to one of pain. He may refuse to pick up his feet or stand still for the farrier. He may become spooky or flighty when he was previously calm.

Learning to notice and interpret all these attempts to communicate, which may indicate ailments as diverse as teeth problems, bruising, muscle strain, digestive issues, parasite damage or psychological stress, is a huge part of winning horsemanship.

Always seek to find and treat the cause, not the symptom.

Knowing when to get expert help, and how quickly, is vital. It is far better to consult one or two knowledgeable sources than to throw a question up on social media and sift through the answers. These days, everyone is a publisher. As a result, there is a huge amount of information whizzing around on the internet. Some of it is pure gold; some is good, sound, sensible advice; but the amount of misinformation, disinformation and wild theories defies belief. This can be entertaining if you know enough to sort the good from the bad and the downright ugly, but what if you don't? Bad advice from amateur veterinarians can increase a horse's suffering. Bad handling or riding advice can also cause suffering and could even lead to injury or death.

> **TIP▶** Always stick to sources you can trust. These include qualified veterinarians, dentists, farriers, chiropractors and the like, who have invested time, money, blood, sweat and tears into obtaining their credentials. The same applies to experienced and knowledgeable trainers and instructors. The other reliable source of information is a good book.

Worming

Parasite control is an important aspect of horsemanship, bearing in mind that there is no such thing as a worm-free horse.

> I once bought a five-year-old ex-racehorse at a country clearing sale. Even though 'Rusty' came with his Australian Jockey Club (AJC) papers, the only other bidder did not look as if they had his best interests at heart, so of course mine was the winning bid.
>
> Rusty was shiny, powerfully built and very fast. Just for fun I entered him in a bush race meeting and discovered what Laura Hillenbrand meant by the words, "To pilot a racehorse is to ride a half-ton catapult". Despite riding in my old all-purpose saddle; we came home with the Baden Lodge Cup and a cash prize!

CHAPTER 4: NURTURE

We began schooling over some low jumps and Rusty was showing promise as an eventer. Then one morning I went out and saddled him up as usual. As soon as I was on his back, I could tell that Rusty was not himself. Not exactly lame, but not moving freely. He wasn't exactly colicky, but he was definitely unhappy in himself. I got straight off again and called the vet. The vet could find nothing clinically wrong then and there, but he took a blood sample and made the ominous prediction that Rusty's case "might be complicated". How right he was.

When the blood results came back, we learned that Rusty had suffered a ruptured aneurism, probably caused by old strongyle damage from lack of appropriate parasite management when a youngster. It was touch and go for a long time, and heartbreaking to see him so terribly ill. If only someone had used an ounce of prevention earlier in his life, we wouldn't have needed the ton of cure that was ultimately required to save it.

Riding Rusty, 1982. Photographer: Jack Pappas

Conventional wisdom used to advocate a regular drenching program with a rotation of chemical groups to minimise worm build-up. However, the cyclic use of wormers, plus chronic under-dosing, have contributed to accelerated chemical resistance in equine parasitic worm populations, much in the same way as "superbug" bacteria are increasingly resistant to antibiotics.

> This problem has triggered an international shift to what is known as 'evidence-based worming'. Jude Matusiewicz (Associate Diploma in Horse Husbandry, Post Graduate Certificate in Animal Science [including Parasitology], Master of Animal Science candidate, member of the Australasia Pacific Extension Network and founder of EvidenceBasedWorming.com.au) is well qualified to comment on the best way to tackle the ever-present problem of such resistance:
>
> "Equine parasitologists and veterinarians now agree that the way forward requires appropriate pasture management and full understanding of the life cycle of parasitic worms. There is a lot of science behind all this but in a nutshell, if there are fewer than two hundred eggs per gram of manure, then we can conclude that pasture contamination will be low and the horse does not currently need treatment.
>
> While an egg count confirms the presence of adult worms, it cannot give an indication of the actual worm burden. Its main strength is in identifying which horses are responsible for the greatest pasture contamination, so that only those horses are treated. My motto: 'Confirm *Before* You Worm', embodies my passion to empower horse owners with the knowledge and technical skills to undertake faecal egg counts on their own horses before considering using chemicals.

CHAPTER 4: NURTURE

> The 'manage and monitor' method of evidence-based worming is attractive because it relies on prevention of infestation and maintenance of natural immunity rather than dependence on drugs and chemicals, some of which have unwanted side effects including killing dung beetle larvae. Dung beetles are our friends! It is not only friendlier to the horse and the environment; it can save you money, especially as your horse numbers increase. Nevertheless, a strategic, targeted approach will require a shift in thinking by horse owners who are accustomed to the chemical method alone."

TIP ▶ Consider acquiring equipment that will let you do faecal egg counts on your own horse's manure, so you can decide when you need to administer a wormer.

If you don't have access to evidence-based worming services, it is still a good idea to worm all new horses arriving at your property and to keep them confined for several days so that the killed worms and eggs can exit their systems before turning them out in your paddocks. After that, you can monitor faecal egg counts to determine when worming should be repeated. If you are meticulous about removing all manure in yards and stables, and also worm your horse again before turning him back out at the end of the competition season, you will greatly minimise the risk of re-infestation of your pastures and keep your horse's worm population at an acceptable level.

TIP ▶ When you do administer a wormer, it is important that you do not under-dose. Establish your horse's weight using scales or a girth weight tape and dose accurately or over-dose by 10 to 15 percent.

No Foot No Fun

In terms of your role in hoof care, if you feed your horse as outlined above, including the provision of a comprehensive multivitamin and mineral formula, then he should not need additional hoof food and the like. Mind you, Rome wasn't built in a day, so if he starts off with poor feet, it will take some months as new horn grows and old cells are replaced for you to see some improvement. In extreme cases, an additional hoof food formula may be useful to optimise healing in the short to medium term. Be patient and resist any temptation to attempt to improve the appearance of the hooves by sandpapering and the like. Such 'cosmetic' procedures are harmful because they weaken and dry out the hooves. Pick out the feet regularly. Make sure they are clean, dry and healthy, with no bad odour or other signs of disease or infection.

TIP ▶ Dressing the feet with a little hoof oil, underneath as well as on the sides, will help with their flexibility and natural water-repelling ability.

Use the opportunity of checking the feet to feel up and down the legs as well, looking for heat, swelling, puffiness or painful spots, along with any little cuts or scratches that might need treating. It pays to head off infection before it starts.

In addition to a great veterinarian and an excellent dentist, you need a master farrier and possibly a chiropractor on your team. Make sure your farrier doesn't 'dump' the toes or leave the heels too long or too short. The front wall of the hooves should have the same slope as the corresponding pasterns, so that they can function optimally with the rest of your horse's conformation.

> *When you find good professionals, treat them as if they were your clients, not the other way around.*
>
> JOANNE VERIKIOS

CHAPTER 4: NURTURE

The Human

Let's talk about you for a moment. How healthy are you, really?

> When I was running the Highborn Warmblood Stud from 1984–2000, my vision was to breed the ultimate riding horse and I made it my business to have the healthiest horses in the country. I spent time, effort and money ensuring that my horses had clean water, good pasture, plenty of exercise, sweet hay and chaff, quality grains, fabulous feed formulas and added supplements. I worked around the clock riding, breeding, feeding, grooming, organising vets, carriers, farriers and dentists – not to mention checking mares and foals at all hours of the night. Oh, and I had a full time job and was competing as a powerlifter... So did I take similar care of myself? Unfortunately not. I knew it, but I didn't do it. Did neglecting my own health have consequences? Of course it did. Fortunately I saw the light before it was too late and now feel better than ever.

With Meiyen and APH Cienta, both in foal to Highborn Powerlifter, circa 1995. Photographer: Jack Pappas

Whether horse or human, being healthy is about feeling and looking your best at any age because what you see on the outside is an indication of what's happening on the inside. Healthy is a sparkle in your eye and energy for another ride or another chore. Healthy is hydrated skin, supple muscles, joints that don't hurt, strong bones and teeth. Healthy shows in the way you move as much as in the way you look.

Our bodies give us feedback, but how often do we listen to them? When you get a twinge, do you pay attention? What about the next time, when the niggle comes back a little stronger? If you have less energy than usual, do you put it down to a big week, a late night, or old age? How often do we really stop to ask ourselves, "What does this mean? What should I do about it? What can I do about it? Who can help me?"

We never plan to get sick, injured, run down, or depressed, but how often do we plan to avoid, if not eliminate, such unfortunate events? Prevention is better, cheaper and usually a lot more pleasant than cure. If you want to die of old age, instead of degenerative disease, you need to take good care of the miracle that is your body. According to a range of scholars and scientists, following just six simple steps will set you up for wellness instead of illness. They are:

1. Eating a healthy balanced diet.
2. Getting enough sleep.
3. Managing stress.
4. Exercising for at least thirty minutes per day.
5. Maintaining good digestion and bowel health.
6. Taking a high-quality vitamin and mineral supplement.

CHAPTER 4: NURTURE

> *"To become successful you must become a person of action. Merely to "know" is not sufficient. It is necessary both to know and to do."*
>
> NAPOLEON HILL

It is important to remember that the body needs a balance of both physical and mental relaxation. For instance, when you are physically tired, it makes sense to relax by resting your body: listening to music, reading a book, or meditating. On the other hand, when you are mentally tired or stressed, the best form of relaxation could be a brisk walk, a ride on your horse or a jog, all of which can serve as moving meditation.

TIP▶ Think of sleep, stress management, relaxation and exercise as essential tasks. Schedule them as such and keep your appointments!

Insufficient emphasis is placed on s-t-r-e-t-c-h-i-n-g before we ride or work out. Flexibility, strength and endurance are all important, but flexibility will go a long way towards keeping you injury-free. The best plan is to warm up, stretch thoroughly, then work out. If you don't know how to stretch properly, ask your teacher, or a strength and physical preparation coach, or a competent massage therapist or physiotherapist. Your body is for life, not just for a lesson or a performance.

TIP▶ If your class or event doesn't include time for stretching first, then try to do it before you go. Your mind, muscles, joints and ligaments will thank you for it!

chapter 5

CONDITION

"When I bestride him, I soar, I am a hawk: he trots the air; the earth sings when he touches it; the basest horn of his hoof is more musical than the pipe of Hermes."

WILLIAM SHAKESPEARE, HENRY V

chapter 5
CONDITION

Conditioning is an art which involves both the external appearance of the horse and its internal fitness for the type of work it is being prepared to do. The condition you put on your horse will depend on how well you manage the steps discussed in the previous chapters in addition to your exercise and flexibility program.

Whether you are preparing for a particular event or series of events, you should plan your conditioning program in advance and put your horse on a timetable culminating in the first important outing. For a horse to be shown in halter classes or presented for breed classification, for example, you would want to allow at least eight to twelve weeks to accustom him to a new regime, teach him the behaviour and skills he will need in the ring, prepare him for some of the sights and sounds he will experience and work on weight, muscle tone and coat. A different routine, a change of diet, more or different exercise, learning new things, being shut up in a stable or yard, being separated from his friends and wearing different gear can all cause stress, particularly to young and inexperienced horses.

Exercise and training are your friends. Horses are large animals that have evolved to be on the move most of the day. As such, they need plenty of exercise. Left to roam freely in a paddock of sufficient size, they will exercise themselves enough to keep their circulation healthy. They can also let off steam or warm up whenever they need to by bucking, playing and zooming about. If a horse is to be kept in a restrictive yard or stable for long periods, he MUST receive adequate regular exercise. This is absolutely vital for his mental health as much as for his physical health.

TIP ▶ Handle this transition period sympathetically and all will be well. If a more experienced horse is available as a companion,

CHAPTER 5: CONDITION

it will give novices both company and confidence so they will adapt faster.

When a horse begins his program of preparation with a hay belly or grass belly, some people try to cut corners by increasing concentrates and decreasing hay, but this 'easy way out' does not pay off in the long run, as you run the risk of creating a sick, fractious or misbehaved horse. The better and more natural way to sculpt your horse's waistline is to exercise the horse by working him for around twenty minutes per day.

Additional benefits of this approach include more contact and therefore more training opportunities; a horse in better and therefore more attractive physical condition; and a horse with a calmer and more cooperative mindset. As a wise person once said, "The horse you get off is not the same as the horse you got on; it is your job as a rider to ensure that as often as possible, the change is for the better".

Your exercise program will of course depend on the sport or discipline in which your horse is to participate. When you plan your conditioning strategy, you will want to take a number of factors into consideration. Foremost amongst these are the age, stage of growth and experience of the horse and the desired psychological, physical and skill changes in response to the conditioning regime. For foals and mares in foal to be shown in breed classes, then self-exercise along with leading practice will probably suffice. Young or unridden horses will benefit from periods of liberty work, lunging or being led from another horse that gradually increases in duration or intensity.

In addition, we need to establish a baseline of suppleness, fitness, soundness and body fat, and make adjustments in view of the time and resources available. We want to give the horse work that he can do, that he enjoys, and that will make him fitter, stronger and more beautiful. We must take care not to overload his mental or physical faculties as we want to enhance willingness to please by avoiding confusion, pain, over training and injury.

Just started under saddle, Highborn Powerlifter is clearly enjoying our first ride outside the yard.
Photographer: Jack Pappas

Riding a fitter, stronger, more mature Highborn Powerlifter at Equestrian Park in Canberra.
Photographer: Jeanne O'Malley

> *"Can I bend him? Can I stretch him? Can I straighten him? And can I collect him? If I can do all of those things, I know I've got a supple horse."*
>
> CHARLOTTE DUJARDIN

The art of your conditioning program is to tailor it to each horse and each event. Conditioning is a dynamic process and you should expect to modify your program as the horse responds. On a daily basis, you will need to decide whether to stick to the plan or to increase or decrease the duration or the pace or the distance travelled or the difficulty of the exercises during each workout. Observe, remember, compare, feel.

Physical Preparation

Like me, Ian King is an author and a former powerlifter. Unlike me, Ian is the pre-eminent trainer of athletes and coaches in the world and has been involved with helping winners from more than twenty sports compete and win on the international stage.

In 1980, Ian started looking for the answer to the simple question, "What is the best way to train?" Finding no-one in the formal education

CHAPTER 5: CONDITION

system who really knew the answer, he chose to keep searching through informal study and practical experience. Athletes were attracted to his quest and by 1986, Ian had more than a hundred national-level elite athletes from different disciplines in his care. For the past thirty-five years he has been helping athletes and coaches to find answers to his question, always striving to serve their highest and best interests.

When I asked Ian for the keys to the physical preparation of equestrians and their horses, his answer was first and foremost to trust your intuition, noting that our upbringing and education condition us to suppress intuition in favour of research. The following is a summary of a fascinating interview:

> "When I was a young man I suffered an injury to the knee. I trusted my highly qualified and respected physical therapists and did certain things to rehabilitate the joint. These training paradigms were the dominant trend in 'science' at the time. My blind trust caused me long-term degenerative changes that I carry for life. With the wisdom of hindsight, I learnt that I should have been more objective in my personal analysis of the decisions, and asked for intuitive guidance.
>
> When I teach this concept, some think I am crazy, some find it intellectually interesting and some apply the teachings practically. I encourage the latter. This means you need to be willing to be non-conformist when your best interests are being threatened. Don't assume that all those in your circle of influence have your best interests at heart. Sadly, ego, dogma and the desire to be in control sometimes result in influences that are not in your best interests. Team sport athletes are more likely to fall for this conformity, and I find it tough to watch when they knowingly concede what they know is best for them to appease a person with power or perceived power in their support team.
>
> Amateur, young and weekend athletes are potentially even more influenced by the desire to conform. Two key areas shape their behaviour and it's rarely for the best. The first is trends. Trends,

I suggest, are commercially driven. They are not there because they are optimal, they are not dominating because they are in the best interests of the end user; they dominate because someone has driven the paradigm for their own commercial benefit.

The second area of influence is what people see higher level athletes do, or what is written about what they allegedly do. Guess what? What elite athletes do is mostly trend-driven also! The only difference is that the trend-driven behaviour is from their physical training consultants. This then reinforces the trend, and everyone wants to follow it.

Stop! Think about it! Be willing to objectively analyse what's best for you. The majority of conformists will tell you to stop 'challenging' the truth, or to stop being 'crazy'. You are being neither – you are simply pausing to reflect, to use the innate natural gift of intuition, before dedicating the value of your time and energy and your future health and performance to the paradigms of the masses.

The first principle I want to stress is that no training in sport helps you as much with your sport as playing the sport. So firstly, if you lack technical skills, get them on the horse. If you lack riding fitness, get it on the horse.

Now there are a few things that you will need to do off the horse, and what they are will be influenced by how advanced a rider you are (qualification) and your specific needs (individualisation). Qualification refers to the implication that you may need more advanced off-the-horse training as you advance on the horse. Individualisation means planning your training based on your personal needs. Group sessions cannot by nature provide individualisation.

If you are a low-level rider, you don't need as much off-horse training, and can get by with lower-level professional advice on physical training. However, as you advance as a rider and believe that improved physical training is an area that would benefit you, then you may wish to seek higher-level professional advice.

As mentioned above, the best way to prepare and succeed as a rider is to ride. That said, off-horse training may be appropriate for reasons including:

- Gaining the strength to support posture on the horse.

- Reducing injuries typical to horse riding, including lower back strain.

- Improving flexibility as it relates to both points above.

- Enhancing the ability to tolerate forces and duration on the horse as it relates to improved performance and reduced injury.

In a nutshell, my first priority for riders in their off-horse training is to do the things that may contribute to avoiding injury, and my second priority is to do things off-horse that have the potential to improve on-horse performance. However, riding is and will always be the most important training you can do!

Now let me give you a crash course in what off-horse training will potentially do for horse riding.

Flexibility Training for Riders

Flexibility is the most neglected and suppressed form of training, yet in my opinion it is the most important form of training you can do. If the primary goal of off-horse training is to reduce injury, then flexibility training is the most important and biggest contributor to injury prevention of all training options. Now, horse riding may not be, in some disciplines at least, as obviously damaging to the body as other sports; however, the more you do a physical activity, the more intensely you do it, and the more years you do it, the more imbalances you will develop in the body. You are building injury potential! Stretching or flexibility training is therefore a must do in all serious riders' programs.

Like all new habits, I want to create permanence in developing and sticking to a stretching regime. Too often, humans over-react in the short-term and under-react in the long-term. You see people get excited, get serious for a few weeks or months, and then quit. I would rather see you under train at first to develop and confirm a new, long-term habit. So here's my suggestion: start with a very short duration, low frequency program. Say a ten to twenty minute stretching program, one or twice a week. Then I expect within a few weeks you will see the benefits and want to do more. Once you internalise the benefits, commitment comes easier!

To support the success of your program, I do expect focus but you can be comfortable. Choose a quiet place, and using a soft surface or mat when lying down, focus on what you are doing. If you prefer music, make sure it is calming music, as relaxing is the key to stretching.

Endurance Training for Riders

Australia is a land renowned for its pride in endurance and many sports in our country have a long tradition of running and similar activities to enhance their sports. The challenge with this is that of all the off-horse training modalities, endurance is, in my opinion (and as reflected in a concept I have published that I call the 'Specificity Continuum'), the one that needs to be done the most specifically to transfer to riding.

Now there is one overriding variable and that is the level of competency or level of qualification in riding. If you are a relative beginner, non-specific running or other endurance-type activities may transfer. However, as you advance in ability on the horse, the transfer and benefits from non-specific endurance

CHAPTER 5: CONDITION

training are reduced, and therefore of less value for you. This is due to specific demands placed on what some call 'peripheral' endurance – the things that are happening at the cellular level in the joints and muscles doing the work.

When we do non-specific endurance training, it can significantly improve our heart and lung – or 'central' – endurance; however, as we improve in our riding ability, this factor is potentially reduced in importance relative to our 'peripheral' fitness. So lower-level riders may receive more benefits from non-specific endurance than advanced riders, who will need to get their endurance adaptations from the more specific options – such as riding! Now at this level, we begin to introduce on-horse variables to enhance the training effect, such as in some cases longer duration riding, and in some cases shorter duration but more intense riding drills and activities.

Strength Training for Riders

The popularity of strength training has been on a fast upward trajectory since about 1990. Few have solved the challenge of successfully transferring strength training to their sport, but in the meantime another challenge has arisen and that is the increased incidence of injury in the sports that have introduced more intense strength training programs. I believe this is occurring because strength training is one of the most potent forms of training, causing the most significant changes. Athletes and coaches get confused between improved strength – which can occur quickly – and improved performance from the increased strength. They are spurred on by the quick gains in strength and so pursue more gains. What is not measured or questioned is how the additional strength changes are transferring. The diminished rate of transfer is often overlooked.

Compounding this is the increased injury potential from developing non-specific muscles and muscle imbalances. So before they know it, new injury patterns are occurring, and no-one knows why. They say the events are tougher now, or other excuses. Imagine if you took the biggest, most powerful horse and put a beginner on it. Not in the round yard, but in a large open paddock. Risky? That's what strength training is to all athletes. Now I'm not seeing this trend yet in riding, but sadly I fear it will occur. The bottom line is that you need to be prudent in your application of strength training. Endurance training may fail to transfer, but strength training has a far more insidious potential.

In terms of improving the strength, flexibility and conditioning for horses themselves, I have long said that most racehorses get better trained and more attention than many elite athletes! The horse industry, especially flat-track racing, has been quite advanced in its training approach.

Here are some specific comments on your horse's physical training.

Flexibility Training for Horses

Dynamic stretching is typically achieved through specific drills to have a horse move in a way or direction that enhances its ability to do so. Static flexibility involves even more human intervention, including you picking up the horse's leg and conducting the stretch for/with them. I have been impressed with the recommendations from the veterinary and related industries about how and why to stretch a horse statically. It's hard work due to the size of the horse, and does need expert guidance, but the information is there. We all know how dependent a horse is on mobility for life, and therefore stretching of the legs and related joints forms a critical part of this program. The next consideration will be the spine. And then there are manual techniques for softening the muscles and other connective tissues. There is so much to be done with those big bodies, but

CHAPTER 5: CONDITION

the exciting thing is the possibilities this offers to improve the horse's performance and reduce their injury risk.

Endurance Training for Horses

This option has perhaps the longest history and can be as simple as having the horse do more distance than it has previously. Now, as you can imagine, there are diminishing returns to any stimulus, so you need to be more creative than this. Fortunately, humans in other sports are learning that doing more endurance training is not the only way to enhance endurance. Human studies are showing that strength training can enhance endurance qualities, and I believe in time it will be confirmed in research that improvements in flexibility also enhance endurance. So the first key to endurance training options is to be holistic in your training approach. Rather than doing all long-distance work, include some shorter duration, higher-intensity work. This is typically referred to in human training as interval work. Rather than doing all long-distance work, include some basic strength and flexibility work.

Strength Training for Horses

The great thing about the horse's strength and endurance training is that it will always have a high degree of specificity in that it will involve the horse's natural movements. The primary way to increase the strength work of a horse is to increase the load on the horse. This may include increasing the vertical displacement of the horse, or changing the angle of the land you ride on, or changing the surface you ride on or in. However, there are implications to all these options and the same holds true for human athletes. The best way to explain this is to ask the question, "What would the impact be on the horse's movement pattern, skills and safety, if I was to do that with the horse?"

Training should not be conducted without these considerations – how it may impact specific performance, how it may impact the injury status. Ideally, you will work this question into the paradigms of your coach, in the context of the desired performance movement patterns. All these training methods need to be reviewed extensively and used prudently. As they say in carpentry – measure three times, cut once.

Once you confirm that the activity will contribute to rather than detract from the horse's performance, and that there are no contraindications, you need to ensure that new methods are introduced in low volume and intensity, and built on progressively from this safe starting point. For example, if you change the ground surface, make sure the changes are only subtle and you are progressive in your training duration. If you choose hill work, start with very small changes in the slope angles as you may be surprised how much training effect can be achieved with the least manipulation of variables, and too much change too soon will increase injury risk to the horse.

Speed Training for Horses

Now a fourth training component is speed work. This component is relevant to the riding disciplines where the speed of the horse between two distances is a performance factor. The shorter the distance between points A and B, the more critical speed work is. Speed work with the horse can be as simple as rehearsing the distances relevant in the discipline. You should manipulate and vary the rest periods, sometimes using longer rest periods in training than used in competition between sprints, sometimes using shorter rest periods. A consideration, and again I refer to my 'Specificity Continuum', is that speed training has a relatively high need for specificity for the training to transfer effectively. This includes distances covered and it also includes surfaces used. Humans fall into the trap of doing their speed work on non-specific surfaces, and find their training fails to transfer fully. They appear ignorant of the specificity needs of surface type in speed work."

CHAPTER 5: CONDITION

If you would like to learn more, you can find Ian King's company offerings at www.KingSports.net or look him up on the web.

Progression

A vital component of any conditioning process is adequate time for recovery, in the form of scheduled light workouts and regular rest days. Monitor your horse's demeanour and appetite for clues that he might need some time off. Measure his respiration and heart rate to track improvements in his fitness.

Always warm your horse up at the walk and trot for at least ten minutes on the lunge or under saddle before beginning a training session. Include some bending and stretching exercises in both directions. Make sure you monitor how he is coping with the workload and stop before he gets out of breath. Always cool down after each conditioning session. Walk your horse until he has stopped sweating, then brush or hose to remove the sweat.

Begin with the end in mind, which is that at the end of the process, you want a horse in better shape than when you began, so develop a conditioning schedule that starts gently and builds. Two or three days of 'artificial' exercise a week is plenty to begin with, especially if your horse is coming off a low base. His heart, lungs and connective tissue should have strengthened after about six weeks of introductory work and you can begin to increase the intensity as appropriate to his age and event.

Remember that you want your horse to last a long time, so maintain only a light training regime for young horses. Horses coming in from a break should also be conditioned slowly, to ensure that their muscles have time to adapt to the increased workload without cramping or tying up and that their bones and ligaments have time to strengthen as well. In England, they refer to this process of developing fitness when coming into work as 'legging up'. It tends to involve plenty of gentle hacking over various terrain, including on some hard surfaces like roadways. After the legging up period, the horse can enter into a synergistic program of ongoing fitness work, suppling work and education. Just like human athletes, horses enjoy exercise and the release of the feel-good hormones known as endorphins probably results in the equivalent of a runner's high and a sense of wellbeing.

Grooming

The conditioning process also entails introducing the horse to bathing and to regular, thorough grooming which will benefit the skin and the underlying muscles. Use a quality, detergent-free shampoo and good conditioner for bathing. Even then, limit the number of times you shampoo your horse to reduce the number of chemicals to which he is exposed.

If the horse is to compete or be shown, now is the time to decide issues such as hairstyles and to prepare the mane and tail accordingly. First of all, find out what rules may apply, if any, and then ascertain what will be the most attractive and practical hair do for your particular horse. Handle the mane and tail carefully to avoid hurting the horse or breaking the hair. You may want to show your horse with a bridle path so his headgear fits nice and flat behind his ears. If so, what length will best compliment your particular horse's head and neck? The length of an ear is a common measurement, but you may decide that more or less is better. Some breed societies prohibit removal of the mane but allow a fine plait instead of clipping a bridle path.

An old-time method that works very well on a horse's under-jaw area is singeing. To do this you touch the very tip of a candle flame to the very end of the long hairs. It is completely painless but each hair will burn like a fuse of dynamite and shrivel up, stopping harmlessly just before it reaches the skin. I used to use this on my ponies with excellent results and they didn't even seem to mind the smoke curling past their eyes or the smell of burning hair.

> **TIP ▶** If you decide to try singeing, choose an area out of the wind where a dropped candle will not start a fire; and make sure you do it about a week to ten days before any important outing, because the singed hair ends will form tiny brown blobs that take a few days to wear off.

CHAPTER 5: CONDITION

For a big job like clipping the body, you will need to use large electric clippers. Unless you have done it before, I recommend that you ask an experienced person to clip your horse for you, while you watch and assist. They should clip against hair to get the right length, then with the hair to get rid of the clip marks, often using a finer blade for the second pass.

TIP ▶ A horse to be clipped must be very clean and his coat must be totally dry, so plan ahead and allow plenty of time. Have a suitable rug ready to compensate for the loss of his natural insulation.

How much hair is removed and from where is very much a matter of fashion and taste which varies from breed to breed and class to class. As a judge, I know that all that so-called superfluous hair actually has a purpose so, while I am all for presenting a clean and tidy horse, I personally do not like to see extreme clip jobs where every whisker, eyebrow and inner ear hair has been removed. As these are the horse's natural feelers and part of his defence system, I strongly believe he should be allowed to keep them. At least two European countries agree with me! The long, stiff whiskers are tactile hairs which help horses to sense the things they cannot see in the blind spot at the end of their noses and around their eyes. When you stop to think that that includes food, water and all the prickly, hard and sharp objects they may encounter, you begin to see how important – and beautiful – these whiskers are.

Plan to take your horse to a small show or event about six weeks into your conditioning program with the objective of treating the outing as a lesson, not a competition. Knowing that he won't be fully conditioned, approach the day as part of your preparation. It is a great way to find out how he will behave in a strange environment. Take note of where more work may be required and celebrate any win or placing as a bonus.

With fellow AWHA Ltd Tour Assessor, Silvia Ahamer, and Heidi Warren's filly, RH Jakkaranda on her first outing, 2015. Eric Lloyd Photography.

chapter 6

Morning Training in the 1890s. Painting by J.V. Blaas (1845 – 1923)

EDUCATE

"He who would learn to fly one day must first learn to stand and walk and run and dance; one cannot fly into flying."

FRIEDRICH NIETZSCHE

chapter 6

Educate

Equine Learning

One of the truly wonderful things about horses is that they are absolutely perfect at doing what they are put on earth to do, which is to be horses.

This means that ancient wisdom will work just as well as, and often better than, modern methods. We humans may live in a digital age but horses do not. When early man wanted speed, horses provided it. When early man wanted power, horses provided it. We still talk about horsepower today, particularly in the automotive industry. Even though they evolved millennia before computers, early man discovered that horses provided the original fast download!

Horses neither need nor want gadgets, gimmicks or apps. They are perfect without our help. Amazingly, though, for such a fast, powerful, defensive creature, they are prepared to help us. This means that we – with our superior abilities in terms of reasoning and planning – need not try to change our horses but instead to learn how to work with them so that our goal becomes their goal, their legs become our legs; our eyes and their eyes focus on the same prize. When you achieve that, you can call yourself a horseman or a horsewoman and you can be very, very proud.

> **When you achieve that, you can call yourself a horseman or a horsewoman and you can be very, very proud.**

The basis of all horsemanship, no matter what the discipline, relates to the principles of dressage, which originated in the training of war horses. Sylvia Loch expresses it well: "Classical dressage is correct for the horse, correct for you, and correct for that moment in time. The horse hasn't changed in thousands of years, neither have human beings.

CHAPTER 6: EDUCATE

We are all ruled by the same physical laws of nature, which is why there is no middle way. Only correct, and incorrect". Similarly, Julie Goodnight observes that, "There are many skills and manoeuvres that people tend to classify as either Western or English. But the truth is horses are horses – their balance is the same, the way they move and the way in which the rider uses the aids for cueing are the same. The appearance of your clothes and tack doesn't really change that".

The horse–human relationship should be mutually pleasurable and rewarding. You know it is mutual when a horse will leave other horses to be with you, even though you are not a horse; even though you bring no treats or feed; even though you may be carrying a halter or a rope or a saddle.

We are lucky because today's horse is very like the horse of yesteryear and the pool of knowledge about how to relate to horses is very deep. We are unlucky because the pool of knowledge is also very wide and it can be hard to know who to trust or what will work. In the end, always remember that, while the perfect horse has yet to be foaled, every horse is brilliant at being a horse.

> *"Horses are made to be horses."*
>
> FRANZ MAIRINGER

TIP ▶ If something is not working out in your relationship, look to yourself, your skills, your knowledge, your attitude, your ambitions and even your calendar. It is never the horse's fault.

All horses who are to interact with humans must learn firstly to trust our species. Do not underestimate the leap of faith they so generously make in doing this, because it is rather like you or me deciding to trust a wild tiger or timber wolf. Accordingly, it is counterproductive to force yourself on a horse. As Ray Hunt puts it, "If you are going to teach a horse something and have a good relationship, you don't make him learn it – you let him learn it".

Paul Belasik makes a similar observation, "It is all subtlety... When we do it right, there won't be much drama. You learn to increase your attention and you train your mind to let more information come to you... You learn to have more patience, you learn to watch, and you learn to let it come to you. To train horses well you have to learn to observe subtleties".

Secondly, horses need to learn some basic ground skills, manners and behaviours. These include acceptance of being touched and groomed all over, standing still, picking up feet, tolerating routine procedures like hoof care, worming and injections and being led, tied up and perhaps lunged and rugged.

TIP ▶ Use the back of your hand to touch a green horse – to him it looks and feels less predatory, less claw-like, than your palm and fingers.

The horse must learn to yield to pressure, which is actually contrary to his natural tendency to brace against it. Pat Parelli calls this the opposition reflex. For instance, when a horse does not respond to pressure applied to the lead rope, he is bracing, not yielding. When he does not move over when pressure is applied to his side, he is bracing, not yielding. When a horse bolts instead of slowing down in response to pressure on the bit, he is bracing, not yielding. Bracing is their default response, their reflex is to oppose the pressure; whereas yielding is a learned response.

> *"Make it a habit to praise when the horse yields."*
>
> NUNO OLIVEIRA

TIP ▶ Opposition reflex can also be used to our advantage. For example, if a horse is lying down and you want him to get up, try pushing him down further. Provided there is nothing seriously wrong, he will soon scramble to his feet!

CHAPTER 6: EDUCATE

Achieve the basic training curriculum as outlined above and constantly reinforce it with mindful regard for the horse, and you will have built a solid foundation for exhibiting your horse in hand. Additional groundwork will then prepare a horse for being ridden or going in harness. Once all the basics are in place, the horse will willingly cooperate with riding and driving. After that, the horse can be worked in an enclosure to fine tune his responses under saddle, so that he understands what is being asked of him and can respond with precision – stopping at a marker, changing gait on command and so on. Pretty soon, the horse will be ready to perform in the big wide world, doing whatever job it is that he has been asked to do.

It sounds so easy when you put it like that, doesn't it? In many ways it is that easy, provided the trainer keeps the horse's psychology and physiology in mind at all times. It is worth it, because a well-trained horse who does his job with a smile on his face will always have a good home. Think of it as making rather than breaking.

Shadamar Golden Challenge, a young Anglo-Arab, looking happy about his first ride, circa 1982. Photographer: Jack Pappas

> *"Nature does not hurry, yet everything is accomplished."*
>
> LAO TZU

Educating a horse is a lot like putting together a thousand-piece jigsaw puzzle, one with a lot of green grass with a few rocks at the bottom of the picture, a lot of blue sky with few clouds at the top of the picture, and a smaller section with some more varied shapes and colours in the middle.

Just as with a jigsaw puzzle, a slow, patient, methodical approach is vital. Start with the corners. Learn how a horse thinks, how he ticks, and the puzzle will begin to fall into place. There is no point trying to force anything; doing that will result in a flawed picture with damaged pieces and you will have to start over again. The temperament of the horse handler is therefore far more important than any characteristics of the horse. It is sometimes easier to train a real, live horse than to tame the wild horses of our emotions, but to do one we must also do the other.

When deciding when and what will be done with your horse and who will do it, remember the old adage, "You only get one chance to make a first impression". Too many people have chosen the wrong breaker, the wrong exercise rider or the wrong groom and have had to live with the consequences and their own regret. Horses are amazingly forgiving, but they also have superb memories, so make lots of enquiries, listen to your intuition, choose very carefully, and stay in touch with what's going on.

I asked Katie Umback (see Chapter Two) what, in her opinion, are the key elements that make up a horseman or horsewoman. Her answer is enlightening:

> "Personally, I think the most important element when dealing with horses is patience. When working with horses, you have to be very patient, understanding, learn to give and take in the learning process, not cut corners and rush anything, because

CHAPTER 6: EDUCATE

> a horse will learn the wrong thing to do a lot quicker than the right thing to do. By being patient, you will build the trust in the horse; if you lose your cool with them they don't forget and become very hesitant then in trusting and cooperating with you. From my experience, anything you do with horses takes time and you have to be consistent and thorough in whatever you are trying to achieve.
>
> I have always been very strict with my horses with what I expect of them but I have always kept my training regimented and been very patient in the process. My main objective is to establish a universal language between the horse and myself. A language we both understand and when you establish this language, you are then on the same page and the horse learns their job and it eliminates any grey areas of confusion. You need clear, black and white communication.
>
> When on the ground with a green horse, I base all my training on natural horsemanship skills. When on the horse's back, I have always based my training on dressage principles and still do to this day; that sets them up and gives them the key to unlock any discipline to go on with."

My first ride on Star did not begin well. He stood like a rock while I was given a leg-up, but then he continued to stand like a rock even when I asked him to move.

Mr Watterson said to start asking for a walk with as little as possible, a mere thought, a gathering of the reins, a change of posture, a squeeze of the legs. Star did nothing. Same sequence again, a stronger squeeze, and then a little kick. Star ignored me. It wouldn't have helped that, due to my size and his shape, my legs and heels were spread over the top part of his broad skewbald back, which was nicely insulated from my efforts by the flaps of a sturdy old Australian stock saddle and a double-thickness checked wool serge saddle blanket. Repeat with a double kick. Star maintained his immobility. Repeat all previous steps and kick really hard. Zero response from Star. I must also say that I was getting very frustrated and inside my head my eight-year-old's brain was saying, "Why bother with all this thinking and squeezing when even the kicking is pointless?"

But Mr Watterson was as patient with children as he was with animals. He was Mr Miyagi to my Karate Kid. Two other things were in favour of me doing what I was told: I had been brought up to respect my elders and I wanted to ride.

Mr Watterson could get Star to move along smartly, so there must be light at the end of the tunnel. Think, pick up the reins, sit up, squeeze, kick, kick-kick, kick-kick-kick. Star flicked an ear in my direction – the beginning of communication! Think, reins, sit up, squeeze, kick, kick-kick, kick-kick-kick. I must have looked so comical.

Mr Watterson produced a short piece of old garden hose. Do it all again, then show him this, he said, demonstrating by holding the hose beside his hip like a sword and then turning his hand so it flicked out sideways. Think, reins, sit up, squeeze, kick, kick-kick, kick-kick-kick, show the hose. Star still didn't actually move his feet, but as his eye followed the hose I felt him sit up, so to speak, and take notice. Alright, said Mr Watterson, do it all again and if you have to, smack him behind the saddle with the hose. Think, gather, feel, ask, demand, insist, reach back and slap him with the hose. Finally, Star moved off.

There's an old saying about giving a man a fish, which will feed him for a day, versus teaching a man to fish, which will allow him to feed himself (and potentially many others) for a lifetime. Mr Watterson taught me to fish. He never once touched Star.

CHAPTER 6: EDUCATE

> He didn't lead him off, he didn't even click his tongue, he never spoke to the horse – only to me. The bottom line was that Mr Watterson was not there to give me pony rides. He was happy for me to ride Star, but I had to do the riding while he went about his business at the stables. So instead of providing a quick fix, he took the time to lay the foundation for me to begin to become an independent rider.
>
> That first day I learned a valuable, golden lesson: do as little as possible, no more than necessary, escalate in stages until the horse offers the correct response, then stop asking, sit tight and enjoy the ride.

Tom Dorrance, one of the fathers of the modern natural horsemanship movement, said, "You feel and listen to the horse. The experience of the results of his response helps you understand for the next time." His brother, Bill Dorrance added, "You can't teach feel, you have to experience it".

Apart from long hours spent with animals from childhood, Maija McLoughlin learnt about horsemanship, riding and stable management from Jennie Loriston-Clarke at Catherston Stud in the United Kingdom, graduated with a Diploma of Stud Management, studied natural horsemanship with Buck Brannaman and taught equine studies in Australia. Because of her remarkable natural ability as an animal trainer, I interviewed Maija about her views on horsemanship. Here is an excerpt:

> "Lose the ego. This is not a competition between you and your horse. Your horse certainly doesn't see it that way. Your horse never wakes up and thinks he's going to make your life difficult today. That's just not how they operate. Sometimes when I was teaching students, I might be four hours on the end of a lead rope and they're saying, "Why haven't you lost your temper? How

can you still be standing here still asking for the same thing?" My answer is because I never see it as a competition or a threat. I see it as an interesting problem and I'm working towards a solution. It's not me against the horse.

You never blame the horse. The horse is never the one responsible for what's going on. Different animals have different temperaments and attitudes, and attributes, certainly. You might train one horse a bit differently from the way you would train another horse because of its personality, but anything the horse is doing, it's doing as a result of what it has learned around people. Some of those things you may be able to retrain, some of them may have been learnt so strongly and so badly by the horse that you can't un-train them and you're better off leaving that to an expert, who may not be able to un-train it either.

For people who are just the average horse person with the average horse, their skills can be vastly improved by paying attention. Watching the horse, being aware of their horse's body language, learning about body language, learning about their own body language. I will say, don't ever see your horse as intentionally competing against you because that never happens.

Possibly, one of the oddest things I ever taught a horse to do was, I once taught a 650 kilogram Warmblood to crawl through a narrow, horizontal gap into a large box on wheels. It literally took three to five minutes to teach the horse to do this. He had to drop his head, turn it sideways, get it through a gap, realise that he could force his shoulders through the gap but it involved lifting his knees up to wither height and turning his chest sideways to squeeze in. He did that because he'd been raised to believe that new things weren't necessarily scary things.

Horses learn how to learn. If they learn in an environment which is comfortable and non-threatening for them, then learning something new is just a matter of curiosity and interest, not a

CHAPTER 6: EDUCATE

matter of fear or threat. Because this horse was already very inclined to follow my orders, I'd been training him for a couple of years, he knew me very well, he was relaxed around me, he knew my body language and hand signals, and when I signalled go forward into this extraordinarily narrow and awkward gap, he just went forward into the gap because that's what he always did. He did what I asked him to do comfortably and confidently.

Maija and her grey Warmblood gelding, McCulloch (Mac), demonstrating finger-tip control. Photographer: Joanne Verikios

Maija and Mac showing mutual respect, trust and understanding. Photographer: Joanne Verikios

Any animal that's learning will get it wrong a number of times before it gets it right, but as long as they're not punished for getting it wrong and you keep asking them, giving them the signal to keep trying, keep doing it, they will keep trying until you stop signalling them. Then they go, "Oh, okay, that's it. I've got it right". It really is as simple as that. The horse learns to keep trying until you stop indicating that he ought to keep trying, and then you give it a reward for that. As long as they've not been frightened in the learning process, they're very willing to have another go.

Really, everything learns through the process of negative reinforcement. People tell you that dogs learn through positive

> reinforcement, but in fact, in order to get it to do what you want it to do the first time, for instance, you're teaching it to sit, yes, you give it a reward, but also, you push down on its bottom when you want it to sit down. That's the negative part of the reinforcement message.
>
> The problem that people have is that they think that negative reinforcement is punishment, and it's a completely different thing entirely. Once people learn how to turn negative reinforcement to their benefit, it works on anything. You can teach an amoeba to move in the direction you want it to move in with negative reinforcement. Really, it's a very powerful learning tool.
>
> The simplest, most basic way to think about it with horses is that when you're riding a horse, you squeeze with your legs when you want it to move forward. The moment it moves forward, you stop squeezing. That's negative reinforcement. It's got nothing to do with punishment."

Sally Swift says the conversation between you and your horse should be, "Ask, receive, give. Ask, receive, give. The give is your thanks". When you learn how to give at the very moment your horse tries, you will find that he will learn much faster and the lesson will stick.

chapter 7

Teaching to Learn

"Remember you must not hurry, and you must not chatter. When you feel impatient you had better leave off, and begin again another day."

J.S. Rarey

chapter 7
TEACHING TO LEARN

To summarise some of Maija's messages, a horse must be taught how to learn and must be treated in such a way that he enjoys learning. That means that you must be patient and persistent. A horse is unable to learn what you are trying to teach him if he is fearful or stressed or distracted by pain. In fact, that is the prime time for learning things you do not want him to know, like pulling back and breaking head collars or rearing over backwards.

"Once you have seen quality horsemanship and are exposed to the things you can do to help a horse be gentle and dependable, then why wouldn't you do those things? No matter what your horse's age, you are going to try to offer him the best that you can. If you adjust what you are doing, he will adjust too; horses have an amazing capacity to make changes. There is always hope." Buck Brannaman

We communicate with horses via aids or cues. Whether natural (voice, seat, hands and legs) or artificial (saddlery, whips and spurs as extensions of the body), aids provide a language by which we transmit our wishes to the horse. Punishment is not part of this language, although, as we have seen above, negative and positive reinforcement are.

TIP ▶ Think of your whip as a wand. Think of spurs as fingers on your feet. Be assertive but gentle.

If your horse exhibits behaviour that you would like to change, a detached and observant attitude on your part will let you analyse why he is doing this. In other words, is it something he has learned, perhaps as a result of less than optimal training; is it a lack of understanding what is required of him; or is he afraid or distracted? Once we have worked out why the horse is doing whatever it is, we can then create an individual approach to begin modifying the behaviour. One method for reducing fear is habituation, which we will explore soon. Another

CHAPTER 7: TEACHING TO LEARN

method, sometimes called counter conditioning, involves replacing the old response with a new response.

For example, if your horse resists flexion, it is not because he is a stubborn weasel, hell bent on sabotaging your dreams or making you look bad. Not at all. Your horse resists flexion for the same two reasons he resists everything else. The first may be that he has not yet been trained to know what you want and to respond accordingly. You may be dealing with a simple case of opposition reflex. The second may be that it is uncomfortable or even painful for him. Or both.

Consider this. Every other day, you do some stretches that help to supple your calves, so both legs are pretty much equal. Then one day you sprint for the bus and strain one of your calf muscles. Try doing the stretches now and getting the same range on each side. It hurts, right? Well that's how it can be for your horse, particularly early in his career under saddle when he might be very one-sided or unbalanced. Just as you would do for your own body, test and measure; see how far you might be able to push things without causing pain or damage, work the position and then let it be. All in good time, your legs will be equal again, and so will your horse become more evenly supple. Even very simple things can be difficult to do: try crossing your arms the other way from usual, or brushing your teeth with your non-dominant hand.

TIP ▶ Your horse's job is to yield to your request. Your job is to understand that your request may be a big deal to him physically (or mentally) and to accept that he is doing his best.

Ray Hunt described it as making the right thing easy and the wrong thing difficult. Antoine de Pluvinel commented that in training horses, one trains himself. In his famous book, *How to Win Friends and Influence People*, Dale Carnegie makes the point that a man convinced against his will is of the same opinion still. The same goes for horses. And Japanese poet Takashima Gyokutoro tells the other side of the story, noting that even the winner of an argument has a hard time sleeping. For a horse–human relationship to be a thing of beauty, we want our horses to be our willing partners; and we want to be able to sleep at night knowing we have treated them fairly.

> *"For what the horse does under compulsion… is done without understanding; and there is no beauty in it either, any more than if one should whip and spur a dancer."*
>
> XENOPHON

When you 'dance' with your horse, somebody must lead and that somebody must be you, not the horse. The leader decides where to go, at what tempo, and what other moves might be layered over the top; the partner follows. In ballroom dancing the couples are in physical contact, which is more like riding; in tribal style belly-dance, the troupe does not touch but nevertheless follows the signals given by the leader, which is more like liberty work. It takes a while to learn the steps and how to relate to one another as a harmonious team. So much depends on your own skills, timing and ability to concentrate.

TIP ▶ Try to be 100 percent mindful of what's going on and 100 percent consistent. It will help if you put your mobile phone away – that's right, no music through your earphones – so you can really pay attention to your horse. If you are on automatic pilot, you might miss something important.

TIP ▶ Always keep your objective in sight and break it down into smaller chunks for your horse.

When you concentrate on what you are teaching and on what the horse is learning, you will not inadvertently reward the wrong thing so often. For example, if you don't want your horse to shy, you should avoid patting him and soothing him and saying 'Good boy' when he is in the process of shying. That is the time to be firm and focussed and say 'Let's get on with it, there's nothing to worry about here'. When you are both safely past the object of terror, then and only then do you reward him. I know, it's easy to say and not so easy to do. But if you work on it with mindful regard, your feel for these things, along with your timing and skills, will improve.

Chapter 7: Teaching to Learn

Pony Club helps to reinforce these principles in young riders and the lively environment and varied activities provide a great foundation for a safe horse. Have you noticed, however, that kids' horses in general tend not to be so spooky? It's not just the pony temperament, it's because children don't see the world in the same way as adults and most don't nanny their mounts in the same way.

Take a Ride on the Wild Side

Children are more inclined to revel in a horse's exuberance, whereas many adult riders have been conditioned to fear it. Whether we are consciously aware of this or not, at a subliminal level we are drawn to horses because they connect us with what is fundamental, elemental and all-powerful.

> *Owning a horse doesn't make you a horseman any more than owning a saddle makes you a rider.*
>
> Joanne Verikios

Early in my former career as an office worker, I identified with a poignant cartoon created by that talented commentator on modern life, Michael Leunig. Mr Leunig has kindly given his permission for me to share it with you here.

> I don't want to use a mouse. I want to ride a horse!
>
> WHAT FOR? IT WOULD ONLY STAMP AND SNORT. IT WOULD BUCK!
>
> YOU WOULD RIDE OFF INTO THE NEVER-NEVER AND FEEL GREAT primitive energies moving under you
>
> YOU WOULD HAVE TO DEAL WITH STRENGTH GREATER THAN YOUR OWN and powerful animal instincts. YOU WOULD BE HUMBLED.
>
> You would have dust on your face. Your eyes would sparkle. You could start to BUCK! THERE'S A SERIOUS RISK THAT YOU MIGHT BECOME MANLY AND NEVER FIT INTO NORMAL LIFE AGAIN. SORRY — NO HORSE!
>
> *leunig*

Luckily for me, I had my horses as well as a mouse! I revelled in feeling those great, primitive energies moving under me, and I had learned to deal with and delight in strength greater than my own, long before mice were connected to computers. Standing a stallion at stud certainly puts you in touch with powerful animal instincts and, oh yes, I was often humbled! Nevertheless, my eyes sparkled through the dust that often filled them and the sparkle soon returned after the tears that sometimes flowed instead. Incidentally, this cartoon also speaks volumes about the conditioning of children to fit in with the world, rather than following their passion.

One of the most amazing things about horses is their wild, raw ENERGY. The energy is always there – calmly contained while grazing, explosively expressed during play, incredibly focussed during mating, madly released when fleeing from danger. We love it. We love to watch it; we love to think about it, people write poetry about it, some of us love to feel it.

Embracing energy and knowing how to use it is what makes up the middle part of the pyramid on the next page. Having established confidence, through communication we work on building cohesion, which culminates in control. Consistency is the key and when it all comes together, magic happens.

CHAPTER 7: TEACHING TO LEARN

WINNING HORSEMANSHIP from BASE CAMP to PINNACLE

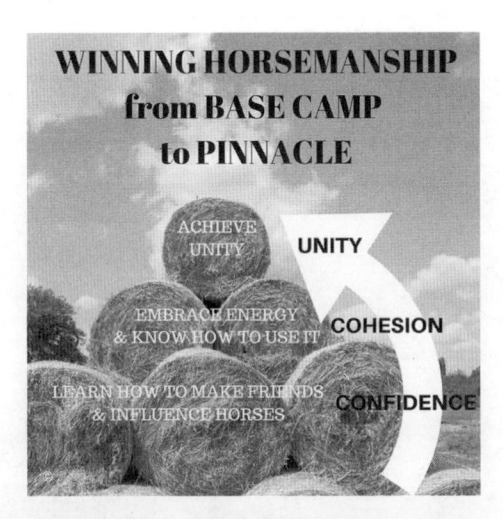

ACHIEVE UNITY — UNITY
EMBRACE ENERGY & KNOW HOW TO USE IT — COHESION
LEARN HOW TO MAKE FRIENDS & INFLUENCE HORSES — CONFIDENCE

The Winning Horsemanship Learning Curve

Many people wish their horses were more like motor cars. You can have a performance car which looks great, standing obediently in the driveway with infinite patience. Everyone appreciates all those 'horses' under the bonnet, but there is no danger of unleashing them until you choose to put your foot down. A horse, on the other hand, is much less predictable and most definitely has a mind of its own. All that horsepower, as exhilarating as it is, does bother some riders to the point where they prefer to stay at a safe pace in a safe place. Maija McLoughlin cites the example of a friend who's been riding for thirty or forty years, rides dressage up to Advanced level and judges to Medium, yet has never galloped on a horse and has never ridden in an unfenced space.

I am certainly not advocating that you gallop hither and yon before you have the skills to stay on without hanging on; or before your horse has the miles under his belt to respond to your aids, even when his blood is up. What I am saying, however, is that galloping is exhilarating, galloping is good for you and galloping is certainly good for your horse, irrespective of what you use him for. In fact, if you want to excel in some sports, you are going to have to get very good at enjoying and controlling the gallop. The beach or the bush are fantastic places to practise.

Fiona Hughes successfully campaigned Highborn Powerlifter in all three Olympic disciplines for his Stallion Performance Testing. Photographer: Jack Pappas

So, when the timing and conditions are right, maybe towards the end of a ride with an experienced friend, try easing up into a nice little hand gallop on a large circle, then compress back to a canter. Repeat. If that goes well, you can gallop a little faster or further, or try it when you are alone. An inspirational image that you might like to bear in mind is the one of movie cowboys streaming across the prairie, their horses galloping flat out, tails streaming behind them, and the riders sitting practically motionless, looking for all the world as if (era permitting) they could pull out a smart phone and check their messages. Or think of a bunch of kids on their ponies, riding flat out, taking each other's bridles off, laughing and having fun. Relax and go with the flow.

CHAPTER 7: TEACHING TO LEARN

TIP ▶ If your horse goes and will not stop or if he wants to share his love of life by throwing in some bucks, use ONE rein to curve and slow him (hold the other rein steady). If you use both reins to try to stop him, he has something nice and solid to brace against and can also jerk you loose more easily too. With one rein applied correctly, he must eventually turn and, as he cannot run as fast in a circle as he can in a straight line, he will slow down. Moving your weight assertively to the rear and pushing your feet down as if you were applying the brakes in a car will also help to wear off some speed.

TIP ▶ A hill is an excellent ally when your horse has more energy than you need. Even the fittest horse will eventually tire of the thrill of galloping uphill. It won't be long before he learns that the gallop is just another gait and that you call the shots.

I stopped riding Star when Beauty came to live with me, although I still visited Mr Watterson and hung out at his stables, which were just two doors down from Beauty's first agistment paddock.

At five years old, Beauty was younger than Star and she had done stock work but little else. She arrived with her own bridle and on the bridle was a type of curb bit known as a Spanish snaffle 'because she's a bit hard in the mouth'. I really didn't know what that meant and our first few rides in a small yard (with close supervision) went well. I was delighted to find that Beauty would move off at the slightest pressure – so different from Star. Of course you know what's coming next. It was time to ride in the big paddock and go a bit faster.

To begin with I didn't have a saddle. I rode in, or rather on, a child's old leather pad with a felt lining and clogs instead of proper stirrups. We walked, we trotted, we cantered. Two things happened at once.

The pad began to slip to one side and I discovered Beauty wouldn't stop. Stopping Star had been almost too easy, because the moment I stopped riding, he would revert to his sloth impersonation. Beauty, on the other hand, seemed to go faster and faster as the pad slid down her side, and me with it. Thump. I fell off. Beauty stopped immediately and nuzzled me like a foal. I was thrilled to bits because it was my first fall and I had been told you needed eight falls before you could consider yourself able to ride. Only seven to go, woohoo! I was also rather pleased that Beauty had stayed with me, instead of continuing her orbit of the paddock.

Saddles were expensive but a brand new one arrived soon after (thank you again, Mum and Dad). It was a glorious, black all-purpose saddle made in Brisbane by Edward Butlers and unlike the pad it was shaped so it would not slip.

Back to the paddock, saddle and all. On my own. Walk, trot, canter, more cantering, whoa Beauty, faster cantering… Two paddocks away, Mr Watterson heard the hoof beats and climbed up on his fence to find out what was happening. I didn't see him but I heard him yell, "One rein, not two! One rein! Turn her!" Well, that was a revelation. As we spiralled towards the centre of the paddock, Beauty slowed down and at slower speeds she was easier to stop. "Thank you, Mr Watterson," I panted. He waved and disappeared, leaving me to digest my latest lesson. Eventually I learned to communicate with Beauty so well that I didn't even need a bridle and saddle, let alone a Spanish snaffle.

Circles and curves are comforting, both to us and to our horses, because moving our bodies in wavy lines is fluid and natural, whereas moving in straight, rigid lines requires more muscle tension. So circles are easy and calming while straight lines are more difficult, challenging and exciting.

Experiment with these concepts for yourself, first by moving your hands or feet from side to side or up and down in a straight line; then in circles. Which feels better to you? Remember this exercise and be aware of the extra effort required by your horse when you work on his straightness. When he tries to go straight, even for just a stride or two at first, reward him with a return to circles, serpentines and spirals. Leave the rectangular arena with its straight sides and right-angled corners and go riding outside or play with your horse in a round yard.

TIP▶ Concentrate on asking your horse to go forward, obediently and rhythmically, before asking for straightness, impulsion and cadence.

As your skills improve, you will need to do less and less to achieve more and more. Just as it takes years to become an overnight success, it takes effort to make something appear effortless.

> *Just as it takes years to become an overnight success, it takes effort to make something appear effortless.*

Give Your Horse a Job

Horses love to have a job to do and seem to derive genuine satisfaction from doing it.

Think of the following examples and reflect on whether the horses know what their job is, do it without complaint – indeed with enjoyment – and exude an air of responsibility and dignity:

- A pony in a Riding for the Disabled program.
- A draught horse pulling a plough.
- A cutting horse matching a cow.

Now let's ask ourselves what are the common characteristics? What fundamental ingredients are present in the above situations? Well, we have a horse in a given environment, certainly not his natural environment;

performing a task that is generally not his natural inclination. We also have a horseman (volunteer, farmer or rancher), who has set up the task for the horse, organised the location and equipment, and indicated that the horse should begin. The horseman will also communicate pace, direction, when to change and when to stop. And we have something for the horse to focus on, in the form of a child or a straight furrow or a cow.

Horse and horseman work together in harmony, the child has a beautiful experience, the field gets ploughed, and the cow is separated from the herd. Then it's time to rest or begin a new task. It is a nice picture isn't it? The volunteer holds the lead rein but does not drag the pony around, the farmer may hold the reins but is just as likely to tie them onto the plough and use voice commands alone, the cowboy sits as still as possible with no contact with the horse's mouth and follows the horse's every lunge, duck and weave as it maintains total focus on the cow. There is no resistance, no shying or shirking and everyone is happy.

On this occasion, Powerlifter's job was to stand still while I stood on him!
Photographer: Jack Pappas

CHAPTER 7: TEACHING TO LEARN

My point is that once a horse understands what his job is, has been trained to do it and is trusted to get on with it, he will do that job with enjoyment. Waldemar Seunig describes riding as "the dialogue between two bodies and two souls aimed at establishing perfect harmony between them". Is that the kind of harmony and unity that you see and feel when you lead your horse or go for a ride?

It is clearly achievable, so how do we get there? The three key factors are:

1. Knowing what is required (i.e., having a job).
2. Being trained to do what is required.
3. Being trusted to do what is required.

> *When I think of a riding horse, I believe that his first duty is to keep himself between his rider and the ground.*
>
> JOANNE VERIKIOS

In order to give your horse a job, you have to design it for him first. After all, if someone came to work for you, you would outline their task or tasks, wouldn't you? In some workplaces they provide employees with a written duty statement.

When I think of a riding horse, I believe that his first duty is to keep himself between his rider and the ground. His second duty is to stop if for whatever reason he occasionally fails at his first duty. Simple, yes. But fulfilment of these duties needs to be learned because they are directly contrary to his instinct, which is to get predators off his back and put the greatest possible distance between himself and the predator in the shortest possible time. His ability to transcend this instinct is at the core of the nobility of the horse in his relationship with our own species.

Your first job is to create a 'circle of safety' within which your horse will feel safe and protected. When he knows that he can trust you, he will look to you for guidance and assistance when the chips are down, rather than relying on unthinking instinct.

Sometimes horses amaze us by taking on a job all by themselves and fulfilling it magnificently. For example, they have carried countless injured riders home – staying underneath them and going at a pace that would not dislodge them from their backs – or even dragging them along the ground by the reins, something they would not have enjoyed but did nevertheless.

In essence, when they accept you as their leader and understand that you have a vision which they must follow; their job is to do whatever task you set until further notice.

What does this mean? Obviously, it means different things at different stages of the horse's training and/or your development as a horseman; as well as at different phases of your relationship.

For example, let's say you are a farmer and your horse is an experienced station hack. You need to check a boundary fence. The horse's tasks include the following:

- Come to be caught.
- Lead easily and respectfully to the saddling area.
- Stand politely during hoof picking, grooming and tacking up.
- Stand still while you mount.
- Remain standing still until you indicate you are ready to move off.
- Move off at the gait and pace and in the direction you choose.
- Maintain that gait, pace and direction until you say what should change – gait, pace, direction or all three.
- Perform turns on the forehand and turns on the hindquarters as part of getting the job done.

CHAPTER 7: TEACHING TO LEARN

An experienced partnership would not even think about what is happening. Their journey would simply flow from departure to return.

Broken down into chunks, however, it might go something like this: Mount up, walk a small circle, head for the gate at the walk. Halt at the gate, get in position (moving forwards or backwards or moving the forehand or the hind quarters) so the rider can unlatch it, ride through, get in position so the rider can close it. Head off at a walk in the required direction. The horse keeps walking until asked to trot. Maintain a trot until asked to canter. Canter and keep cantering, jumping a small log en route. Come back to a trot and turn left towards the creek. Slow to a walk and slide down a steep bank to the creek, walk through the water, canter up the opposite bank. Here is a beautiful stretch for a gallop. When asked, the horse breaks into a gallop. When asked, the horse comes back to a canter. When asked, the horse trots. When asked, the horse walks. We have now reached the fence line to be checked, so the horse walks along it, stopping wherever the rider wants to take a better look. Halt at a broken section of fence. Remain motionless while the rider dismounts and removes some tools from the saddlebag. Stand quietly with the reins looped over a sapling until the work is done. Stand still to be mounted. Set off for home at the pace and via the route dictated by the rider. The rider offers a halt at the creek so the horse can drink. The horse accepts and would also like to splash and roll in the creek. The rider says 'no playing, let's go' and the horse obeys. They canter up the opposite bank, then trot, and then walk the rest of the way home so the horse can cool off. The horse walks smartly but does not pull, reef or jig jog. Back through the gate, back to the saddling area. The horse stands still during dismounting, unsaddling and hosing off, then leads calmly back to his paddock where he is released.

How can we summarise this? Assuming a horseman is a competent and accountable leader, then a horse's job is to obey the horseman. His obedience is reflected by his unquestioning willingness to be or go where he is directed to be or go and to maintain the requested level of immobility/mobility and direction until a different request is made. Assuming the horse knows what is required, then the horseman's job is to delegate those duties to the horse. This means trusting that they will be carried out and being ready to correct if they are not.

> *"If I have always worked honestly, my horse will carry me to the end of the world."*
>
> E.F. SEIDLER

When you have developed a relationship with your horse that results in such obedience and trust in your judgement – and sharing of your goals – no matter what else is happening, then congratulations, you have truly achieved a winning partnership.

chapter 8

PREPARE

"To horses, every day is a new day to survive. It's a natural instinct. They don't think of the past or the future, only the present. So in terms of trying to teach your horse or build a special bond, patience is the key to every stall's door."

SHEIKHA HISSA HAMDAN AL MAKTOUM

chapter 8
Prepare

Show Proofing Your Horse

We've all seen those motivational posters about living in the moment. The past represents guilt, the future represents worry, so just be present here and now and everything will be alright. Sounds good, but it's easier said than done – if you're a human.

Horses, on the other hand, do not so much live in the moment, as live the moment. Provided that the moment is a calm and unthreatening moment, they are very Zen. However, it doesn't take much to upset the proverbial apple cart and, often faster than the eye can follow, our horse morphs from tranquillity and reason to full-on fight-or-flight mode.

The good news is that there is plenty we can do about this, including learning to see it coming and taking preventive action. But first, why does it happen?

> Let's go to a hypothetical horse show and watch one scenario unfold. You arrive a bit late but there is still half an hour before your first class so you send your sister off to pick up your number while you get the horse ready. Unloading goes well and he has miraculously managed to stay pretty clean so he just needs a bit of a wipe over before tacking up.
>
> At this point, your horse is in the moment – he is in 'here we are standing beside the float at a horse show again, no big deal' mode.
>
> You, on the other hand, are in a semi-trance state. Yes, you are physically present at the showground but you are still annoyed about running late, meaning you have to rush your warm up and preparations, even though it was your fault that you forgot to pack your jacket and had to turn around and go back for it.

CHAPTER 8: PREPARE

> You are wondering what else you might have left behind. You are also worried that your horse isn't in prime condition for this show and that your plaits aren't as neat as some that just walked past. The horse with the superior plaits has quarter marks too and they look great, but you won't have time for that.
>
> This little mixture of guilt and fear is keeping you preoccupied as you take your horse for a quick walk around to stretch his legs and check out the surroundings. Being a finely tuned herd animal, he picks up on your mood, especially the fear element. Your horse thinks, "Fear?! Hmm, this showground looked okay, but there is obviously something to worry about because my human is frightened. Good grief, she was right, there it is; I am so OUT of here!" And in the blink of an eye you have a rope burn and a loose horse.

In this kind of scenario, you have loaded the gun – with your thoughts and body language – and the trigger could be anything at all: bunting stirred by the wind, a child with a balloon, another horse playing up, a noise. What 'it' was doesn't matter, or rather, in all likelihood, it would not have mattered had you not inadvertently put the horse on high alert.

Now I'm not saying that horses don't take it into their heads to spook and shy for reasons of their own. They do that too. But in improving our horsemanship, we want to reduce the probability of the unplanned and the unforeseen.

So what can we do about it? If our thoughts or body language can influence our horse in a bad way, hey presto, they can influence our horse in a good way. We 'just' need to control our thoughts, emotions, movements, and facial expressions. It will take preparation, practice and persistence, but when we learn to master ourselves, we can enhance our horsemanship so that our ability to control our horse under all circumstances is far greater.

> **To paraphrase James Allen, as a man or woman thinketh, so is his or her horse.**

It is distressing to see horses of all ages who spend the entire show wide-eyed and fearful at the smorgasbord of new and exciting things to see, hear, smell and experience. Unless your horse always lives in a very busy environment, there is so much more going on than at home that it can become overwhelming. The presence of other horses can be very stimulating, especially for colts and horses that live alone.

The opposite issue is the horse who is loaded in the float and towed away from his special friend. If he suffers from separation anxiety, it can seriously ruin your day! Not to mention ruining his day. Thousands of years of survival instinct tell our horse that being separated from the herd is a very bad idea. Alternatively, he may think he's being weaned all over again. Either scenario is traumatic and we want to avoid that.

Then there are the horses who cope well with the general atmosphere but lose the plot when the public address system fires up or the applause starts. Or the horses who strenuously object to having a deadly ribbon tied around their neck. Or horses who have never encountered other livestock and suddenly find themselves within sight or hearing and smelling range of pigs and alpacas.

If we look at things from the horse's point of view, we can see that even the smallest, quietest outing is very different from the peace and predictability of the stable or paddock at home. While some horses cope better than others with change, it is not always easy to predict how they will react and having a horse that is constantly dancing around, rearing, pawing, and neighing in your ear rarely improves your enjoyment of the outing.

What can we do? The answer is to be prepared. Basically, you want to introduce all the fun of the fair to your horse before you go anywhere near a show. In the words of Tom Roberts, you want those scary sights, sounds and sensations to become 'old hat'. This may involve time,

CHAPTER 8: PREPARE

patience and creativity on your part, but no significant expense. All of the strategies below will make your horse calmer, safer and nicer to be near, whether you compete or not.

Some of my weanlings 'discover' an umbrella. Photographer: Joanne Verikios

> **"Think of each of your daily schooling sessions as a story unfolding."**
>
> JANE SAVOIE

TIP ▶ Introduce anything new with great tact and do not move on until your horse is calm and confident.

As horse owners, we could take a leaf out of the training methods for guide dogs. Have you ever seen those cute little Labradors in their puppy coats? They are being socialised and introduced to the big wide world by their puppy raisers. Since horses are somewhat bigger and stronger than dogs, and less welcome in the shopping mall, it's our job to bring the world to them through simulation. Let's start with some of the typical things we may see at a show or event.

TIP ▶ Try to set things up so your horse encounters new things from what HE considers a safe distance. Reduce the distance as his comfort increases.

Bunting: get a strip of bunting (or just use pieces of old fabric or plastic bags). Start by attaching your bunting to the farthest fence from where your horse normally hangs out. Leave it there until he ignores it whether it's fluttering or not, then move it to another fence, then another and so on. You can also lunge or work your horse in an arena with plastic bags tied to the rails. When he ignores the bunting no matter where it is or what it's doing, you have made significant progress. Flags and pinwheels are also good training aids.

Meeting other horses: if you don't have other horses coming and going, it will pay you to take yours somewhere where he can observe this phenomenon a few times. Think about what's available in your area. Perhaps you can lead or ride him past other horses until he stops reacting to them, or put him in a safe yard or stable for a day or so at a busier property, or take him to watch Pony Club from a safe distance (for both you and the kiddies). When his behaviour changes from reacting to merely noticing, you have created a safer, more confident horse.

Clapping, music and announcements: noise is pretty easy to deal with. Just turn on a radio, quietly to begin with, then, when your horse is in a safe environment, turn up the volume now and then (that section at the end of a live concert where people suddenly burst into thunderous applause is perfect). A good place to do this for the first time is actually in the paddock or in a round yard, so the horse can run away if he wants to. Live or recorded race calls are also great for simulating PA systems. Before long, clapping, music and random loud voices will be old hat and he will no longer feel the need to expend the energy required to leave. Repeat this exercise from time to time, until your horse stops reacting. Play him some reminder pieces a day or so before the show. While he is eating and feeling good about the world is an excellent time for a bit of musical and vocal accompaniment.

Ribbons: this one is also easy. First of all, make sure your horse enjoys having his head touched and his neck rubbed, stroked and groomed.

CHAPTER 8: PREPARE

Once that is established, walk up to him and tie an imaginary ribbon around his neck. So far so good? Now have someone else approach with an imaginary ribbon. When he's happy about that (and it might take a few advances and retreats by the other person), repeat using a piece of soft rope as a ribbon. Pretty soon you'll be able to use a piece of coloured fabric, or an old ribbon. If you don't have any ribbons yet, I'm sure you'll be able to find someone to lend or give you one! When your ribbon training is looking solid, switch things up by repeating the exercise with your "judge" or "steward" wearing a floppy hat, a flowing skirt or maybe approaching with a limp. Think of some of the presentations you've seen and use your imagination to ribbon-proof your pony.

Highborn Powerlifter on the way to winning Champion Warmblood at Canberra Royal Show, 1992. Photographer: Jack Pappas

Rosettes: the same applies as for ribbons, except that your horse needs to get accustomed to having a large round item with streamers on it attached to his halter or bridle. You can simulate a rosette by simply tying a wide ribbon in a bow on his headstall or bridle. Make sure that you also get him used to being led around wearing his ribbons and rosettes, and let him know that he is a hero and you are very pleased with him. When he is comfortable with these decorations, you could even have an assistant play some applause and marching music to reinforce his success! Many horses learn to love applause and will accept it with great pride.

Practise riding with one hand so you can carry a trophy too.

What else might you need to do? Like the puppy raisers, treat all the events and phenomena of daily life as opportunities to socialise and desensitise your horse.

Get your horse used to working in the rain and to people using umbrellas. Rub his body all over with a closed umbrella until he is enjoying it. Then open and close the umbrella slowly from a short distance away and keep doing this with rhythm until he is relaxed. Progress to moving the open umbrella over and around him.

TIP ▶ Keep the environment safe. Neither you nor your horse should be in danger of getting tangled in or injured by the items you use to desensitise him.

It is essential that first of all, he learns to have confidence in you as the fearless and dependable herd leader; secondly, that he learns to yield; and thirdly, that he be trained to live in the real world, because you simply cannot manage or predict everything that might happen.

> This really came home to me at the Yass Agricultural Show in 1989, where I had taken my then four-year-old stallion, Highborn Powerlifter, to compete in the Warmblood classes.
>
> On the way to the ring for a led class, we had to pass groups of people. Very much a stallion, with an inclination to show off his magnificence at all times, Powerlifter shamelessly became taller, wider and even more arch-necked in front of an audience.
>
> Even so, he was leading beautifully until he suddenly stopped dead. "Walk on," I said. No response. I gave a tug on the lead rein. He didn't budge. So I looked around to see what was bothering

CHAPTER 8: PREPARE

> him and noticed that he had a calm but worried expression that was directed rearwards. "I can't move because of THAT," he seemed to be saying. I found out what it feels like to be simultaneously horrified and grateful, because behind my stallion was a red stroller containing a golden-haired toddler who had grabbed a tiny handful of Powerlifter's tail.
>
> Meanwhile, the child's mother was chatting away and had no idea that anything untoward was happening. "Excuse me", I said, "we need our tail back." Mum must have been a country girl because she sized up the situation, released the tail and, after a quick "Sorry about that," continued her conversation.

Allow your horse to become familiar with children, dogs, cats, chickens, goats, sheep, cattle, wheel barrows, mowers, tractors, cars, push bikes, motor bikes, trucks, paper etc., as the opportunity arises. The younger a horse is when he has an opportunity to overcome his fear of unusual things the better, but horses of any age will benefit from desensitisation. Whether on the ground or in the saddle, always maintain the attitude that these things are a quite natural part of life, trust that your horse will follow your lead, and be prepared to work things through if they bother him.

- **TIP ▶** It will help both of you if you consider this process a game, not a chore. Never forget that your attitude is everything, so make it fun for both of you.

- **TIP ▶** Make sure your horse is used to the sound of different mobile phone ring tones (starting on low volume and working up) and car horns too.

- **TIP ▶** Use the horse's herd instinct to your advantage by working in a group or having a more experienced horse set an example and show the novice horse that everything is alright. A great example of this is the way mares teach their foals that thunder and lightning are not so frightening. Another is the use of an experienced horse as a travel companion during Junior's first ride in a float, trailer or truck.

TIP ▶ Look for and reward the smallest of wins. Arrange things so the horse wins a lot! Praise him when bravery is shown, never force a stimulus or an obstacle on him and never punish resistance.

TIP ▶ If things are not going so well, persist with great patience until you can find a good place to leave the exercise, stop, praise the horse and put him away or do something he is already familiar with.

Reiner Klimke advises us that, "Whenever a horse has learned a new movement or a new aid in its basic form, the rider should give him a break and deliberately ride something else for a few days or weeks. When he returns to the movement, he will notice how much more easily the training will proceed". Mark Rashid notes that, "Horsemanship is nothing if not an exercise in timing. The less obstacles we put between request and response, the closer we get to what I consider to be the ultimate horse–human relationship – in short, it's when the horse learns how to respond less to our physical cues, and more to the connection we offer them through feel and intent".

Your mission is to introduce your horse to varied, unfamiliar situations in the most tactful possible way. That means making it interesting rather than terrifying, appealing to his innate curiosity rather than his fight-or-flight reflex and developing his ability to use the left side of his brain. Instinct tells the horse, "don't just stand there, do something!" Our goal is to help him to think rather than react and to rely on us for guidance as to what his response should be. We want his default position to become, "don't just do something, stand there".

> *"At each stage of work the horse must be taken to his limit, but never over the limit."*
>
> WALTER ZETTL

chapter 9

Becoming a Champion

"The most difficult thing is the decision to act, the rest is merely tenacity."

Amelia Earhart

chapter 9
Becoming a Champion

As athletes in a team of two, you and your horse will ultimately need some form of outside assistance if you want to compete. Even if your goal is pleasure riding and you already have a level of competence, you will benefit from some lessons and new exercises to keep you and your horse fresh and responsive to each other.

Because it's what we learn after we know it all that counts, it is vital to our growth and progress that we get input from various sources. In all walks of life, even the best in the business have coaches, mentors or advisors. A typical progression might run along these lines:

- A beginner has a teacher or an instructor to help them learn basic skills.

- An intermediate athlete has a coach to help them practise the basic skills and develop new ones.

- An advanced athlete has a coach to help them consolidate their skills and move towards mastery.

- An elite athlete has a coach to help them hone their skills and master their craft.

Most horses are started under saddle by an experienced rider and at all subsequent levels they may be entrusted to a professional trainer to familiarise them with their sport or discipline, the equipment, specialist manoeuvres and the like, and to make them easier for the owner to handle and ride. In some cases, the horse is further along their relative scale of experience than the rider and can teach the latter a great deal. Alternatively, riders can benefit enormously from training sessions on so-called school masters, so that they can get the feel of a movement before attempting it on their own, less experienced, horse.

CHAPTER 9: BECOMING A CHAMPION

A word of warning: there is no shortage of people of varying degrees of skill and integrity who offer their services. Some are true professionals with experience and a wonderful reputation to back it up. Some have good skills but less experience; others have plenty of experience but questionable skills. As an owner and horse lover, you must do your own due diligence before entrusting your horse's mind, body and spirit to another person. Google them. Ask lots of questions. Visit their premises. Inspect their credentials. Get references and try to view other horses they have handled.

At the same time, stay open-minded as to method or style. Ignore the silo mentality that is often adopted by others and learn from everyone (even if it's sometimes a lesson in what not to do). The basics are the basics; there is no need to confine yourself or your horse to a particular method or style, nor are you obliged to stick with just one trainer or coach.

If you don't have access to a coach or trainer, it will pay dividends if you can find someone to watch you ride and give you feedback in real time. A person who can describe what they see and what changes occur as a result of adjustments you make is far more valuable than a mirror, but a mirror is an improvement on no feedback at all.

Such feedback does not take the place of what your horse tells you with his body and what you feel through yours, but it is a very helpful adjunct and you will benefit from even an occasional session. An experienced person is preferable, but any 'eyes on the ground' are better than none. Having someone watch you work with your horse also changes the energy and the atmosphere, which can be useful when preparing for competitions.

An accountability partner can also be invaluable, just to hold you to what you said you would do and to keep you on track as you pursue your goals. They don't even have to be 'horsey' or be present when you work with your horse.

Other resources available to you are lessons, clinics, seminars, websites, webinars, books, videos, podcasts, attending equestrian events as a spectator or viewing live-streamed competitions from all over the globe. Video your own rides and note your horse's movements and reactions to your requests in the replay.

While a coach or trainer can take you a long way, a lot will depend on your desire to help yourself and find your own answers. You need to be willing to work things out for yourself and take action accordingly.

Ian King (see Chapter Five) knows a lot about the essential qualities or personal attributes of a winner from his work with Olympians and other elite athletes:

> "The first lesson I want to share is that winning comes from within. The only one that determines if the athlete or horse has the ability to win is you and/or the horse. As trainers and coaches we provide the one percent that may be missing, but if you add one percent to a mule it's not going to win the local derby!
>
> The second lesson I have learnt is that champions and courage come in all shapes and sizes. Too often I hear criticism that Athlete X is too tall, too short, too skinny, too large and so on. It doesn't matter what anyone else thinks. Winners come in all shapes and sizes, so forget about stereotypes and other people's opinions!
>
> The third point I want to touch upon is ignoring the limiting beliefs about superior backgrounds. Some blame their genetics, some their equipment, some their funding. We can all find excuses. However, champions come from positions of adversity also. It's not about the adversity you face. It's about what you are willing to do to rise above your adversities!
>
> The most important thing I can share with you is that you can choose to be great, whatever that means for you, and you have the tools to find answers to the questions: 'What is the best way for me to train? What is the best way for me to train my horse?' You have your intuition, and you should use that as you search for the answers."

CHAPTER 9: BECOMING A CHAMPION

The fact that you are reading this book indicates that you are in the top five percent who are prepared to do your own research and further learning – congratulations!

> I wanted to be able to vault onto Beauty bareback, like the Indians did in 1960s TV shows like "The Lone Ranger". The trouble was that I was small and Beauty was too tall for me to mount without a stirrup.
>
> Down at the back of the paddock were some trees with low hanging branches. I felt that if I could hold Beauty's mane with one hand, then spring up and grab hold of one of the branches with the other, I would have a better chance. It took a bit of experimentation to get pony and branch in just the right position. Then I had some work to do convincing Beauty that it was okay to stand still while I swung on her mane like Tarzan with one hand, launched myself at her withers and then, if I managed to get high enough, pulled a branch into her opposite side with the other hand. So as not to hurt her, I used to take my riding boots off and do these sessions barefooted.
>
> I slowly got better at co-ordinating my attempts and Beauty got more and more laid back about the whole exercise. I suppose I also built a bit of specific strength in the relevant muscles. The day I finally pulled it all together, hooked a foot over her back and hauled myself aboard, was one to be remembered! Eventually, I was able to use the branch less and less until the moment arrived when I could swing up, just like an Indian, anytime and anywhere I wanted. Yay! It was an attractive point of difference with the method used by my contemporaries, who mounted bareback by flinging their midsection over their pony's back, then wiggling and twisting until they had a leg either side and could sit up. I became so good at it that I could use "my" method to mount any horse whose withers I could reach, just as long as there was a bit of mane to hold.

Part of taking responsibility for your own life, your own progress and your own horse is to do what you know and feel to be right. This can include holding the line, even when someone like a coach or a trainer has other ideas. Remember that no-one has your and your horse's best interests at heart to the same degree that you do.

> *I like the order Jim Rohn proposes in this piece of advice, "To solve any problem, here are three questions to ask yourself: First, what could I do? Second, what could I read? And third, who could I ask?"*

When you come to forks in the road of your horsemanship journey, your question will contain or create the answer, so keep asking questions of yourself as much as of others until the answers you find add up to solutions which are very specific to you and your horse. It's all about deciding what is right, not who is right. Don't just rely only on your instructor because, human nature being what it is, they may feel compelled to give you an answer even when they don't really have one.

You also need to ask the right questions when you are communicating with your horse. According to Pat Parelli, "If your horse says no, you either asked the wrong question, or asked the question wrong". Ultimately you want to be able to rely on yourself, ably informed by feedback from your horse. The best answers are usually within you already. You just need to find them.

CHAPTER 9: BECOMING A CHAMPION

Pat Parelli makes a point at a seminar I organised in Canberra in 1993. Photographer: Jeanne O'Malley

Sending Fear to the Rear

We have discussed the fight-or-flight response with regard to our mounts, but how about for us? Just as for horses, this response has less actual utility in the modern world than it did at an earlier stage of our evolution. That doesn't stop it influencing our behaviour, however, even though fear is completely imaginary. That's right. Danger is real; there is no doubt about that. But fear – say the fear of entering a show ring or dressage arena – is all in our minds.

We can control our home environment up to a point, but we cannot control the environment when we go out, nor can we control the actions of others, so it is imperative that we control what we can, namely our own reactions.

You probably know that fear begins in the primitive, reptilian part of the brain, the same limbic system that is geared to our survival. It is the part of the brain that tells us when we are hungry, drives us to find a mate, attracts us to a warm, sunny spot and warns us away from dark places where anything could be lurking. The same limbic system tells a horse it is not a good idea to get into a horse trailer or a stable, or to trust his weight to something that might give way or trap his legs.

Fear is at play when perfectly nice people turn into the equestrian equivalent of a Bridezilla. They become a Ridezilla: a rider whose behaviour is seen as demanding or unreasonable, the -zilla suffix being derived from the movie monster Godzilla.

> **They become a Ridezilla: a rider whose behaviour is seen as demanding or unreasonable, the -zilla suffix being derived from the movie monster Godzilla.**

A horse learns to overcome his fears and so can we. Understand that when your lizard brain prepares you for fight or flight, it sets off a number of biochemical changes in the body. Adrenaline is pumped to your muscles in order to provide the rapid response necessary to run away from the sabre-toothed judge, sorry, tiger; or fight it off. You start to sweat in order to provide evaporative cooling, because your brain knows that all that action will make you hot. Your breathing becomes rapid and shallow, again to help you get out of danger fast. You also develop a very keen and particular focus on the point of danger, just like a horse goggles at something that has frightened it.

So that's the reality – what can we do about it? How can we keep our cool and get in the zone where peak performance is possible, indeed inevitable? We can bar fear from our performance, using the things we can control. Can we control adrenaline and sweating? Not without a lot of practice. Can we control breathing and focus? Yes we can! So our formula for managing fear is:

Breathing + Attitude + Relaxation = BAR

Apparently there are people who are so afraid of public speaking that they would rather be in the coffin than giving the eulogy. If you are one of them, then these techniques will improve your performance in

CHAPTER 9: BECOMING A CHAMPION

that regard too, which could be very handy for your victory speech and media interviews.

Breathing deeply is the first thing to do. This is actually nature's way of telling you that you are safe (you have survived the tiger attack and can breathe easily again). So allow three deep breaths to the count of four in, hold for the count of two, and then exhale fully, to the count of six out. Inhale all the way into your lower lung, so that your diaphragm pushes your tummy out. Try it now. How do you feel?

Now do it again and try this. After the first hold, as you slowly and completely exhale, relax your shoulders. Feel them drop. Feel your shoulder blades sliding down your back. After the second hold, as you slowly and completely exhale, relax your jaw. Feel your lips soften, allow your tongue to drop. After the third hold, as you slowly and completely exhale, relax your forehead and all the little muscles around your eyes. Roll your eyes upwards a couple of times.

Not only will this quick, three-deep-breaths technique help to calm you, if you do it around your horse it will have a positive effect on him too. You might want to do the eye rolling with your eyes closed, just out of consideration for any onlookers, but you can do everything else with your eyes open.

TIP ▸ Deep breathing dissipates adrenaline. It can change your life.

Attitude is very important to managing fear. Your attitude will be much better if you have done the work required for a good performance at the level at which you are competing. It goes without saying that if you are unprepared, it will not help your confidence. For this reason Silvia Ahamer, former Austrian Junior Show Jumping Champion, Upper Austrian Eventing representative and international Warmblood breeder, advocates working at least a level higher at home than in competition.

I do appreciate, though, that it is also possible to feel underprepared even if you are 100 percent ready! The key is mental preparation in the form of habitual visualisation and virtual performance, well in advance of the event. Visualise perfect execution of whatever it is that your event requires. Anticipating that everything will go beautifully is an important part of attitude.

TIP ▶ On the big day, boost your confidence by walking at a brisk, more purposeful pace than you normally would. Breathe deeply as you walk and feel the adrenaline leaving the body.

Research shows that the habit of cultivating a positive attitude and practising positive self-talk helps to reduce your stress levels, improves your holistic health and enhances your capacity to perform to your maximum potential. The key to breaking bad habits or creating new habits is consistency. Keep at it every day, do not let it slip, and before long it will become second nature.

Relaxation will flow from correct breathing and attitude. Can you concentrate when you are relaxed? Absolutely you can. In fact, just like your horse, you will learn more, faster; retain more and perform better when you are in the zone of alert relaxation.

To illustrate this, we only have to think of a frightened, reactive horse. When he is in fight or flight mode, he will learn nothing except what stops the stimulus. If he is running away, he will run as far as he thinks necessary to escape. If he is pulling back on his halter, he will either learn the exact amount of force required to break free, or he will learn that stepping forward relieves the pressure. If he is trying to get a predator – real or imagined – off his back, he will buck and twist and even rear over backwards until prey and predator part company. On the other hand, if he feels safe he will be calm and attentive, capable of learning and remembering.

TIP ▶ Everyone learns better when they are having fun.

> *"A cheerful frame of mind, reinforced by relaxation... is the medicine that puts all ghosts of fear on the run."*
>
> GEORGE MATTHEW ADAMS

chapter 10

Groundwork

"And indeed, a horse who bears himself proudly is a thing of such beauty and astonishment that he attracts the eyes of all beholders. No one will tire of looking at him as long as he will display himself in his splendour."

Xenophon

chapter 10

GROUNDWORK

Groundwork is the foundation of everything you do with your horse. It helps you to get inside your horse's mind to an even greater extent than can be achieved by riding him.

As a judge, assessor and classifier, I see a lot of horses shown in hand as well as under saddle. Some of them are presented very well, but others are let down by small mistakes and inadequate training that can easily be addressed. You are responsible both for your own performance and for the performance of your horse. Conversely, your horse is not responsible for your performance. It is up to you to ensure that he is working to his greatest potential.

What a judge wants to see is the horse moving forward with impulsion, swing and rhythm at all gaits. They also expect the horse to stand still long enough for them to look at it in sufficient detail to do it justice. A horse can only carry itself properly in the ring if it has been taught to focus on the handler and if the handler allows it to show itself to advantage. The handler must:

1. Control and exhibit the horse at the walk and trot as well as when stationary.

2. Provide the judge with a clear view of the horse at all times.

3. Look where they are going.

4. Be constantly mindful of safety.

These factors apply whether you are an entrant in a huge class at a Royal Agricultural Show or a single exhibitor presenting your horse for classification. Let's break these down, examine some common mistakes and make some suggestions for success. A horse which is to be shown in hand must be taught three things, all of which flow from basic training:

CHAPTER 10: GROUNDWORK

A. To stand perfectly still.

B. To walk and trot on command.

C. To allow a judge or judges to approach it and examine it closely, including opening its mouth, picking up its feet, lifting its tail or running their hands over its body and legs.

Teaching to Stand

The younger a horse is, the more latitude it will be given by a judge. For instance, a foal will not be expected to stand still and pay attention for very long at all but a mature horse should maintain his immobility until asked to move.

Like anything, we begin our training in standing still by making the right thing easy, the wrong thing difficult, and rewarding the slightest glimmer of understanding.

It helps to halt our horse in a corner to begin with, so that moving in two directions is blocked by the fence and you are blocking another. We deliberately ask the horse for the halt, tell him to stand, let him know he has done well after a moment of immobility and then we very deliberately move him off again. At this stage we don't worry about posture or foot placement, we only want immobility. One thing at a time. Through reward and repetition, the horse will soon be standing for a little longer each time in the familiar corner. When he understands what you want, use another corner, and then mix it up with halts in the corners, halts along the fence and eventually, halts in the open.

*Highborn Powerlifter strikes his signature pose in Canberra.
Photographer: Jack Pappas*

Once halting and standing are reasonably established, you can start to ask for the correct position, as set out in the guidelines for your breed. Some breeds are shown standing square, others are shown in what is called the open position, so know your rules and train your horse accordingly. Simply lead the horse into the open position. With the square stance, you can teach your horse which foot to move by applying subtle pressure on the rope or halter and then using body language. Ask him first to stand still, then to stand with his front legs square, then with his hind legs square and so on. Persist patiently until he gets it right. As soon as he does, let him be, releasing pressure on the lead and praising him quietly. Ask him to hold it for longer periods, just a fraction longer to begin with; allowing him to relax briefly in the desired position and make a fuss of him before you cue him to walk on.

Calmly repeat the procedure if the horse moves before you want him to. Always stop the lesson on a good note and before the horse gets fed up.

CHAPTER 10: GROUNDWORK

> *"Recognise the smallest change, the slightest try."*
>
> RAY HUNT

Pretty soon your horse will reward you by moving into the right position by himself. Then you can work on refinements like teaching him not only how to stand still but also how to display his head and neck, again depending on breed requirements.

- **TIP ▶** Do not try to hold the horse in place. Instead, let him find it and make it the most comfortable place to be.

- **TIP ▶** Do not pat or rub the horse too much during these lessons, as you don't want to teach him to lean, nudge or rub on you in the show ring. He should maintain a respectful distance.

- **TIP ▶** Talk to the horse during training but reduce reliance on voice commands over time so that you don't need to say too much in the show ring.

Teaching to Lead

The horse must be trained to walk and trot when led with the handler positioned on the near (left) side of the horse, closer to its shoulder than its head, so that the horse's head and neck are visible in front of the handler. The correct position for showing off the horse is also safest position for the handler. In this position, the handler can simultaneously control the forehand and the hindquarters, with the added advantage of not obscuring the head. The lead rope or reins are held in the handler's right hand well back from the horse's chin. Experiment with a length of rope that is approximately a third to a half of the horse's neck length.

A Haflinger stallion and his handler show their paces at the annual Warendorf Stallion Parade, Germany, 1998. Photographer: Joanne Verikios

TIP ▶ Do not hold your hand too low, because that will make the horse carry his head too low. If you are showing a tall horse, you may need to hold your right hand higher than feels natural for you. The loose end of the rope or rein is held in your left hand, but never coiled around it.

If a whip is carried (also in your left hand), the horse needs to accept it without fear and respect it without overreacting. Flicking at your horse with the end of the lead rein is not recommended. It makes you look unprofessional and unprepared but more importantly, because it is far less precise than a tap with a whip, it can touch the horse in a ticklish place with unexpected consequences. It also tends to make you twist to the rear of the horse, which causes the horse curve into your space, losing his line, crowding you and possibly treading on your feet.

TIP ▶ It is better to carry a whip and not need it, than to need it and not have it.

Probably the most important thing for any exhibitor – handler or rider – to do is to look straight ahead. I see so many people looking at their

CHAPTER 10: GROUNDWORK

horse or at the ground while they lead or ride. The horse mirrors the direction of their gaze or loses concentration and looks at something more interesting. In a led class, the two of them move crookedly and sometimes bump into each other as they proceed around the ring. As a result, they miss markers, the handler's hat may get knocked off and the general impression is untidy. In a ridden class, the horse often becomes over-bent. When you look straight ahead and focus, really focus, on where you are going, your horse will look where you are looking and partner with you in a far more harmonious way.

> **TIP ▶** Keep your eyes up and look where you are going. Don't look at the horse while you are leading or riding it – that is the judge's job!

When you begin halter training your horse at home, don't worry at first about his head carriage or other niceties. Just concentrate on asking the horse to move forward and straight with a calm and obedient demeanour, using lots of positive reinforcement when he does what you want. Use a fence to help the horse to lead straight, then move away from the fence when he knows what it required. As with teaching your horse to stand still, repeat your leading lessons in different locations.

A very important lesson is to teach the horse to turn away from you. This simple little secret is one of the things that separates the professionals from the amateurs, who are used to turning the horse towards them and then have trouble when asked to do a led workout to the right. The magic ingredient is yielding. When your horse yields, you can direct his forehand to turn away from you, first by touching him – you may need to physically push him over at first – but pretty soon you can use hand signals and body language without touching him, until you get to the point where, when you change the direction you are looking in, it compresses the imaginary bubble of air between you and the horse responds.

Ideally, your horse will be taught to lead as a foal, although any age is a fine time to start. As a bonus, once you have the foal leading well, you won't have to bother to lead the mare because she will follow her foal far more closely than some foals follow their mothers! A judge will make some allowances for lapses in behaviour, but a well-mannered youngster will always present a good picture and will also impress as having a pleasant temperament.

> We used to introduce foals to yielding by picking them up as soon as possible after birth and holding them off the ground until they relaxed in our arms. The next step was to accustom them to the concept of following a human like they would follow a mare, not with a halter but by looping a long, thick, soft rope around their forehand and hindquarters, in a figure of eight which crossed at the withers. I would hold the cross-over like a handle and with a bit of practice your foal became like a suitcase on wheels, nicely manoeuvrable in any direction.
>
> The loop around the chest stopped the foal from leaping forward and taught it to yield to pressure on the chest and neck. The loop around the backside stopped the foal from ducking backwards and taught it to yield to pressure on the hindquarters.
>
> The sensation of ropes along their sides also helped them to accept reins, girths and rugs later on.
>
> The whole arrangement allowed for a lot of finesse as the foal adapted to this comfortable harness, because I could cue them in all directions with a turn of the wrist and reward them with cessation of pressure just as easily. When the lesson was over there was no unclipping or untying to worry about as the rope simply dropped to the ground.

Leading practice can be reinforced when the young horse is a weanling and so on throughout their lives. Work in all directions: circles, straight, and diagonals. Don't look at the horse, especially when you want it to change gait. Look ahead. And always find a good point to stop, even if you only achieve one or two strides. You can ask for more in subsequent lessons.

CHAPTER 10: GROUNDWORK

Teach the horse to go forward when you are leading him. The horse should walk purposefully, as if he has somewhere to go and is looking forward to getting there. At the walk, he should march along at the pace dictated by the handler without rushing, dawdling or jig jogging. At the trot, the horse should flow forward on command and maintain the pace set by the handler without one party dragging behind or getting ahead of the other. This means, of course, that you must be able to run fast enough and for long enough to allow the horse to show his paces to advantage, sometimes in heavy going like deep arena sand.

> **TIP ▶** If you do not have the necessary skills, fitness or physique, you may prefer to engage someone who does, to exhibit your horse for you.

One of the most common mistakes handlers make is to walk or run directly at the judge at the completion of their led workout. This is because the judge has probably said to come "straight back to me". However, savvy exhibitors know that leading directly back the judge is done so the judge can watch the horse's legs from the front. If you aim yourself at the judge, the horse will move to the inside of the required track, meaning the judge has to move sideways to see what they want to see and then faces the risk of being run over by horse, handler or both.

> **TIP ▶** Create a tidy, professional picture by aiming your horse at the judge and then veering slightly to the left so the two of you pass safely to the judge's right.

Leading necessarily involves stopping too, so practise until you can halt smoothly from a walk or a trot. Then turn to face the horse at a forty-five degree angle to the shoulder and ask it to stand up. Why at an angle and not in front? Those familiar with the television series *Get Smart* will be aware of the Cone of Silence. A horse does not have a cone of silence, but he does have two Cones of Invisibility – one directly in front and one directly behind him. The effect of these cones is to create blind spots. We need to know about them, because people or objects appearing suddenly from a blind spot can startle a horse and his reaction can sometimes have disastrous results. People who show in western style halter classes call the front cone the danger zone and spend as little time in it as possible.

TIP ▶ Standing to the side, where the horse can see you at all times, makes it is easier for him to pay attention.

Led horses also need to be able to back up on command, so teach your horse to yield in that direction too. The judge may wish to assess their soundness or you might need this skill to maintain your position in a line up.

TIP ▶ Remember that the younger the horse, the shorter the attention span. The same goes for older but green horses. You will achieve more in three training sessions of ten minutes than you will in an hour, so teach like you feed, little and often.

TIP ▶ Teach him to keep his attention on you so that he is waiting for your commands and does not have an opportunity to miss or ignore your cues.

TIP ▶ If you don't know how to keep your horse's attention, a good natural horsemanship trainer can help.

Treats and Mistreatment

I do not advocate feeding treats as a reward during basic training. Your horse is not a dog and is not motivated to perform in the same way. Furthermore, the use of treats can lead the horse to expect and then demand them, including under circumstances where it is inconvenient or unprofessional to provide them. A more or less constant stream of treats can lead horses to nip or bite from a sense of frustrated entitlement.

> *"I have come to the conclusion that it is actually a form of mistreatment to love horses so much that you spoil them."*
>
> LYNN REARDON

CHAPTER 10: GROUNDWORK

Do not think that treats will make your horse love you. Horses love other horses and they even love stable mates like cats, dogs and goats, none of whom ever feed them treats. They will value the bond of companionship and teamwork they share with you far more than a piece of carrot or apple – when you have earned that respect by providing company, leadership and fun together. Treats have their place but if care is not exercised they will actually make your horse disrespect you. He is too big and potentially dangerous for that, so make a treat an occasional event. If you put it in the feed bin your horse will love you just as much and respect you more.

TIP ▶ Never use a treat as a bribe.

TIP ▶ Do not let your horse explore your pockets and never offer food to a horse by holding it in your own mouth.

Leading and Showing Exercises

The following exercises are easy to set up and will help you and your horse to focus on obedience and direction while having some fun at the same time. They will also get you used to looking ahead to where you are going; a subtle change that will make a huge difference to your horse.

The effect you want to visualise is a narrow mountain track. Here's your chance to give your horse a job and channel 'The Man from Snowy River', but from the ground, not the saddle. First, you need to mark out your training course. Paint lines on the ground, or use some poles or other safe markers to lay out a winding track. Keep it fairly narrow, say no more than fifty centimetres wide. About twenty metres in total length should be sufficient.

> *Make it a game, not an ordeal, and practise until you can complete the course without either of you putting a foot wrong.*

The course can follow whatever pattern your imagination suggests, bearing in mind that you are simulating a narrow ridge with sheer drops to the right and left! You will want to have a couple of right-angle turns and a couple of hair pin bends. Get some friends together and have a mini competition, just to make it more interesting. Your challenge is to lead your horse along the winding ridge without him pushing you over the edge or falling down the cliff himself. Make it a game, not an ordeal, and practise until you can complete the course without either of you putting a foot wrong.

When you're master of the trail, work on the snail: spiral out to a large circle, then spiral back in again. Change directions. Do this at the walk until your horse is paying attention and following your body language in and out. Then do it at the trot. Then alternate walking, trotting and backing up. There are many variations on these themes, with and without the assistance of poles or ground markings.

TIP ▶ Practise walking, trotting, backing up, turning your horse away from you, moving into position for inspection by the judge and standing motionless, until your horse knows exactly what you want.

Speaking of the judge, you may be surprised by how many inexperienced horses are disconcerted by a judge scrutinising their every move with an eagle eye. This awakens their inner prey animal, because while they may be semi-convinced that you won't kill them and eat them, they don't like the way the judge is appraising their body parts. Again, the answer is habituation, so expose your horse to as many different people as possible.

TIP ▶ While you have your friends together, take it in turns for one of you to be the judge and practise doing the kind of workout required by the events you plan to enter.

Free Schooling and Free Jumping

Some events also call for horses to be assessed at the walk, trot and canter when free in an enclosed arena. Lunging is quite good preparation for

CHAPTER 10: GROUNDWORK

this but your horse will also benefit from a few experiences completely loose in an arena so he knows what is required of him. Once the novelty of finding his gears has worn off a little, you can get him used to moving around at the walk, trot and canter, as well as being caught again. To this end, your horse needs to be familiar with and respect aids like lunge whips, rattles, plastic bags on sticks and the like without being frightened of them.

TIP ▶ When showing foals loose, remove the halter altogether or make sure they are used to it and it fits symmetrically or it will affect their movement, straightness and concentration.

Other events include free jumping where again, preparation is essential if your horse is to acquit himself or herself with confidence and style.

> When I prepared Highborn Powerlifter for Colt Selection, I did not have an arena or even a suitable paddock to teach him free jumping, but it was something he had to learn. My solution was to work him over jumps on the lunge. In addition to lunging on a circle, I also set up a small straight section where he could jump two fences in sequence. My jumps were pretty basic; just poles and wings with another pole leaning against the inside wing so the lunge line could travel up and over without getting caught. I started low and slow with the poles on the ground; gradually working up to the minimum height he would have to jump on the big day.
>
> Well, it may not have been orthodox but it worked beautifully. Not only did Power jump like a champion, scoring nines out of ten for his free jumping and free movement, he enjoyed himself so much that he kept circling the arena and entering the jumping lane again and again of his own free will. While the ground crew were working to raise the jumps, someone even had to shoo him away from the lane until they were finished. As soon as the jumps were ready, he returned to his fun.

When the classifiers had seen enough, he came to be caught when I called him. I was a very proud owner-breeder that day and thrilled when he was named Premium Colt.

WINNING HORSEMANSHIP TRAINING SCALE

UNITY
COLLECTION
STRAIGHTNESS
IMPULSION
ACCEPTANCE & CONTACT
RHYTHM
COMFORT & RELAXATION

The Winning Horsemanship Training Scale

chapter 11

Teamwork

"The art of communication is the language of leadership."

James Humes

chapter 11

Teamwork

In their book *The 10 Day Turnaround – How to Transform Your Business Virtually Overnight,* Spike Humer and Darren J. Stephens discuss the concept of committing to doing whatever it takes: "When we make this personal vow to ourselves and others to create camaraderie, movement, and motivation, it brings about a sense of unity and commitment not often found when things are assumed or often implied. Great leadership means candid communication, not just delegation."

What does that have to do with horsemanship? Two words really jump out at me. Those two words are unity and communication. Your horse needs to understand that you will do everything in your power to keep him safe. If you can communicate this, then he, in his own way and to the best of his ability, will do the same for you. Mind you, mutual trust is not forged overnight. It takes hours, days, weeks, months and years to build such a relationship but once it is in place, magic can happen, because then you have unity and unity is priceless. The legendary Tom Dorrance titled his book *True Unity*.

We take many things in the English language for granted, but when you think about it, one of the first steps in a horse's education is learning 'to lead'. It would be more accurate, given the nature of the relationship, to say that we are teaching the horse to *accept being led*, as it is the human who will (or should) be doing the leading. We also use 'lead' ropes to facilitate this process. By definition, we lead and the horse follows. We can also lead our horses from the middle (as riders) and from the rear (as drivers). Horses readily accept all these variations because none of them is so different from what happens in a herd situation, with a lead mare in front, a stallion maintaining momentum from the rear and the herd in between. No matter how or where we lead our horse, we have to take responsibility for the outcome and we must be able to lead with authenticity and accountability.

CHAPTER 11: TEAMWORK

> *It's team work that makes the dream work.*

It's team work that makes the dream work. To operate truly as a supreme team, the individual members must care as much about each other's success as they do about their own. In a team of two, horse and horseman, the leader who is effective in communicating not only direction but a sense of purpose and a clear end goal with tact and empathy can inspire remarkable respect, loyalty and co-operation in a horse.

> Consider, for instance, the Walers of the Australian Light Horse who carried their riders on a charge into Beersheba. It was the first cavalry charge in Australian history and the conditions were horrendous. This is how Melbourne writer Frank Dalby Davison described it in his 1933 prose epic, 'The Wells of Beersheba'.
>
> "Under the saddles there was a world of courage. At that hour, on the plain and in the distant hills, three columns of horses were moving out from camp. The weight of man and gear rested on backs still tender from carrying their burden through the previous night's march. Twelve extra pounds of rations and corn weighted them down tonight. (They knew the difference!) When the column moved it might be going three miles or thirty, for all the horses knew. Feed, water and rest might be waiting for them at the end – or might not. They had a double hazard to carry as well as a burden. Sustained by comradeship between horse and horse, and by a strange trusting comradeship with the men they carried, they set themselves to the unknown.

> ... A wave of subtle excitement swept through the mounted ranks and communicated itself to the beasts they rode. Saddle-worn, parched and overloaded, the horses knew by the alert bearing of their riders that unaccustomed action was at hand. Weight might have fallen from their burdened bodies. They tossed their heads and fidgeted nervously from hoof to hoof as if fresh from their home paddocks.
>
> ... The pace quickened as horse laboured with horse to gain the lead, and horse laboured to keep stride by stride with his neighbour. Nostrils reddened, eyes widened, jaws gaped, and tossing heads flung spume to the air. Not one of the horses, alone, could have stood the pace and the weight for half the distance; but each, like his rider, was possessed of something beyond himself."

Then there are tales of human bravery and equine understanding in competition.

Australian athletes Bill Roycroft in the 1960 Rome Olympics and Gillian Rolton in the 1996 Atlanta Olympics, both injured, were nevertheless able to win gold medals for their teams and country.

> On the last day of the Three Day Event in Rome, Australia had a problem. While Laurie Morgan and Neale Lavis were going well, Brian Crago's horse was lame and Bill Roycroft, the fourth member of the team, was in hospital due to a nasty fall the day before.
>
> Bill's horse, Our Solo, had landed on him after flipping over at an obstacle made of pipes. Though concussed, forty-five year old Bill gamely climbed back on board and finished the course. He was then helicoptered to a hospital outside Rome. Having been sandwiched between his horse and the hard Italian earth had caused a broken collarbone and soft tissue injuries, leaving him bruised and battered and in severe pain. If Australia was to win the team event, however, three horse and rider combinations needed to finish all three phases of the competition.

CHAPTER 11: TEAMWORK

On show jumping morning, Bill announced that he was leaving the hospital. The doctors refused to discharge him. When he insisted, they countered by confiscating his clothes. When he threatened to leave in his underwear, they finally allowed him to sign a document taking responsibility for his own safety. Back at the stadium, Bill was so stiff and sore that he could not even get dressed by himself. He was lifted onto Our Solo's back with one arm strapped up. Someone put the reins in his good hand. A very stiff rider and a very noble horse negotiated each of the twelve show jumps, culminating in a clear round and clinching team gold for Australia.

I was only four years old and our family did not own a television set when Bill Roycroft triumphed in Rome, but that had all changed by the time Gillian Rolton represented Australia in 1996.

Gill and the grey Peppermint Grove had already won team gold in Barcelona in 1992. I will never forget watching the drama of their cross-country round at Atlanta. The combination was looking good until Peppermint Grove fell and they parted company. Unknown to anyone, including Gill herself at that point, the fall had caused a broken collarbone and broken ribs. She remounted and continued, despite being unable to use her left arm. It was horrifying to watch horse and rider fall again at the water jump. Soaked through but undeterred, Gill waded out, remounted and finished the remaining three kilometres, clearing fifteen more fences at a gallop.

An ambulance, not a helicopter, took her to hospital. She bravely refused painkilling drugs in case she was needed for the final team show jumping round the next day. As it turned out her team mates Andrew Hoy, Phillip Dutton and Wendy Schaeffer had ensured that she did not have to ride and Gill won her second Olympic gold medal.

Bill Roycroft and Gill Rolton showed amazing grit; an attribute that you need to become an elite athlete; and their team spirit shines through like sunbeams piercing a cloud.

I also give massive credit to their mounts. Our Solo and Peppermint Grove did not take advantage of their riders' impairments. Not in the least. Like the Walers at Beersheba who, tired, sore and thirsty, swept into battle; they too shared the vision, carried their badly injured riders over a dozen jumps or more and got the job done. Why did the wonderful Walers, Our Solo, Peppermint Grove and countless other noble horses, whether famous mounts or unsung heroes across all the continents, not behave like naughty ponies and try to dislodge their vulnerable passengers when it would have taken so little to do so? Why did they not refuse the cross-country obstacles or show jumps or, for that matter, duck out when confronted with trenches full of enemy soldiers hell bent on shooting or bayoneting them?

Yes, herd instinct, alluded to in The Wells of Beersheba, undoubtedly played a part during the cavalry charge, but Our Solo and Peppermint Grove performed alone. As Warren Bennis said, "Leadership is the capacity to translate vision into reality".

The critical factors binding all three stories are leadership and teamwork, through communication, which created unity.

Leadership + Teamwork + Communication = Unity

> *You do not have to be an Olympic rider to achieve unity, but it would be difficult to become an Olympic rider without it.*
>
> JOANNE VERIKIOS

You do not have to be an Olympic rider to achieve unity, but it would be difficult to become an Olympic rider without it. During my own encounters with equestrian Olympians, I have been impressed by their

CHAPTER 11: TEAMWORK

sportsmanship. In the riders' dining room, the night before the cross-country phase of the 1998 World Equestrian Games (WEG) Three Day Event, the then Bettina Overesch finished her dinner and called out as she was leaving, "Goodnight everyone and good luck to you all for tomorrow"!

With English Olympic gold-medallist, Captain Mark Phillips, and Bernd Bucher from Germany in Pratoni del Vivaro, Italy, 1998. Photographer: Barbara Bucher

Just a few days before, whilst in Rome for the WEG dressage and show jumping, I had the unexpected pleasure of meeting Bill and Mavis Roycroft. I had chosen a restaurant and requested a table for one. The owner asked if I would like to sit with some other Australians and ushered me to a table where an elderly couple were looking at the menu.

Well. To be in Italy for the WEG was already pretty good, but to meet one of my all-time heroes and role models in the city where he had achieved his greatest fame, and to join him and his wife for a meal, to chat about horses, dairy cattle and country life, was a rare privilege.

> *"Dreams come with strings attached: hard work, determination, persistence, compromise, sacrifice and passion."*
>
> DARREN HARDY

Think Like a Winner

When I first started going to the gym, I felt self-conscious and out of place. I was a complete beginner, 'everyone' had more experience, cooler clothes, bigger muscles, less body fat than I did and I thought that everybody was looking at me. It took a while for it to dawn on me that not only were people not looking at me, some seemed more ill at ease than I was – probably because they thought people were looking at them! It seems to be human nature for us to have this reaction of comparing ourselves unfavourably to others, of not being 'enough'.

Once I got over my self-imposed limitations and focussed on my training, I had a lot of success as a powerlifter, 1985–1988. Photographer: Joanne Verikios

CHAPTER 11: TEAMWORK

Animals don't have this hang up. A cat or a dog with an amputated leg doesn't interact any differently from one with four legs. A horse whose mane has been hogged or whose tail has been chewed off above the hocks by his yearling buddy doesn't feel or act any less powerful than before getting the Samson treatment. But we do, and it doesn't serve us. So here are a few affirmations that might help.

You are enough, just the way you are. In fact, you are amazing. Just what's going on in your body, mind and soul without you having to think about it is remarkable enough, but beyond that, you are who you are supposed to be, where you are supposed to be and you are on a journey of personal development (or you wouldn't be reading this book). You may be a novice with horses or a seasoned hand. As Denis Waitley puts it, "every winner was once a beginner" and no matter where you are right now, there is plenty more to learn.

TIP ▶ When you find an affirmation that you like, write it on a post-it note and write it on your heart.

You have choices and the willpower to exercise them. For instance, you may have been riding for a while and have chosen a style of equitation and attire (English, Western etc.), a sport or discipline (reining, cutting, dressage, jumping, roping, hacking, eventing, endurance, Pony Club games, showing, trail riding, vaulting, camp drafting, polo, polocrosse, tent pegging, medieval pageants, carriage driving). You may not ride but love spending time with horses in other ways, perhaps breeding or showing in hand. You may have decided that showing and competing are not for you: you prefer to enjoy horses in a utilitarian role like stock work or farm work, or purely for recreation.

What is wonderful is that these are all legitimate choices and no one is superior to another. The great common denominator is the versatility of the horse and the two things linking all horsemen and horsewomen are firstly, their love of horses and secondly, their need to learn how to win their trust and influence them in order to work as a true partnership.

Me on Cloud and Jenny Hepple on Venus, ready to begin our regular one hour ride to Pony Club. Photographer: T. W. Liesegang

No matter where you stand (or sit) on the ladder of horsemanship proficiency, irrespective of your horse's (or your own) age, appearance, colour or gender, you have so much in common with your fellow horse lovers. Can you control what other people think, of you or anything else? No. Can you control what you think of yourself? Yes. Can you control what you think of other people and whether or not you are judgemental? Yes. Remembering the 'serenity prayer' may help you to accept yourself, your horse, and others, just as they are, with every right to celebrate similarities and differences alike:

> "God, grant me the serenity to accept the things I cannot change,
> The courage to change the things I can,
> And the wisdom to know the difference."

So live and let live, be true to yourself, rejoice in who you are and take that confidence into everything you do. Work on your own mindset

CHAPTER 11: TEAMWORK

before you even think about your horse's headset. Put your hand on your heart and say "I am enough".

> **Work on your own mindset before you even think about your horse's headset.**
>
> JOANNE VERIKIOS

When I was competing on horseback, my great love was eventing. I didn't compete at the highest level, but I revelled in doing my thing and riding cross-country was, for me, the most fun of all. That said, I have enormous respect for all equestrian pursuits because, since horses are involved, they are all beautiful, exhilarating and uplifting in their own right. As an eventer, I also had to put in a decent dressage test and a clear round show jumping, so that gave me insights into both those disciplines. As an avid Pony Club member, I cut my teeth on gymkhana events and mounted games. I rode my own horses and other people's horses in hacking, turnout and equitation. I cherish memories of riding after cattle with my grandfather and trail rides with R.M. Williams.

As a kid with a pony, I entered everything, including events I had no chance whatsoever of winning. For instance, back in the day, piebald ponies were never called in first in the hack ring. That didn't stop me from entering hack classes and, if the entries weren't large, delighting in any placing I might secure. It was enough just to be at the show with my pony. If the judge couldn't see that Beauty was the best pony at the showgrounds, that was his problem, not mine! As adults, we tend to forget that feeling and be harder on ourselves and our horses than is warranted.

How do you define winning? What does success look like to you? How do you feel when you achieve a goal? Which gives you more satisfaction

– the outcome or the process of getting there, the destination or the journey, the laurel wreath or training for the event, the approbation of the crowd or your private satisfaction? There are no right or wrong answers because your definition of winning is unique to you.

We are all familiar with conventional definitions of success:

- Gold medals and blue ribbons.
- Celebrity status and media attention.
- Wealth (or the appearance of affluence).

These things are fantastic ways of keeping score but they only truly represent winning if you also experience joy, satisfaction and fulfilment on the way to the podium. It's not just about the success; it's about having experiences that are worth the accolades.

If, on the other hand, the price paid for success was too high, for example in terms of damaged health, unhappy horses, broken relationships, bankruptcy or trashed reputations, then winning is not the word that comes to mind. As Martina Navratilova counsels, "The moment of victory is much too short to live for that and nothing else".

And while most of us would be thrilled to win even one bronze medal at the Olympics and many would say that even to compete would be reward enough, there are those who are so driven that they would not be satisfied until they had won four gold medals, or broken the world record twice, or whatever criteria meet their personal measures of success.

Ironman champion Guy Leech recommends giving yourself "an unfair advantage" in competition. Guy is not talking about doing anything illegal, he is talking about going the extra mile. Think about it. Most people do a good job, maybe they even make a 98 percent effort. The champions are the ones who put in the extra two percent. Maybe they start earlier, stay later, push themselves harder, eat better, get more sleep, find a mentor, make the sacrifices that others are not prepared to make. They are the ones who reap the long-term benefits because they make their hopes and dreams come true. A champion gives 100 percent.

CHAPTER 11: TEAMWORK

> *"The only problem with success is it doesn't teach you how to deal with failure."*
>
> TOMMY LASORDA

The less obvious determinants of success are more subtle. They are harder to define and impossible to measure. They are, however, universally available:

- Love
- Health
- Happiness
- Memories
- Contentment

My goal is not to tell you what winning is, because that would mean trying to impose my values and world view. It would be a 'one-size-fits-me' exercise! Rather, my goal is to encourage you to think about what winning and success mean to you. I want you to be the arbiter of what is okay and what is not okay in your inner and outer world, because only you know when you have really made it. Why do you have a horse, really? Why do you ride, lead or breed horses? What do horses bring to your life, your spirit and your soul?

It is in the depths of those answers that you will find the meaning of winning and the shape of success. Perhaps you will find that you are already more successful than you thought. Or maybe you will realise that you'll never know unless you have a go.

One thing I know is that you will find it easier to sustain success if you have balance. Not just the kind of balance that helps you to stay on your horse, but the sort of balance that keeps you from having a breakdown or a breakup on the way to success. You've heard of work/life balance. It is also important to have horse/life balance.

There are times, of course, when the best way to win is not to keep score, because if you are preparing for something big, balance will take second place for a while. In her book, *How We Lead Matters: Reflections on a Life of Leadership*, Marilyn Carlson Nelson makes the following observations: "The fact is that being a leader in any field requires discipline, effort, and, yes, sacrifice. It can be all consuming. And during that time, life may not have much balance… Personally, I liken being a CEO to being an Olympic athlete. It's an exhaustingly gruelling yet richly rewarding time when you're at the top of your game. And I ask you, when was the last time you heard an Olympic athlete complain about work/life balance?"

> *"If you can dream it, you can do it. Always remember that this whole thing was started with a dream and a mouse."*
>
> WALT DISNEY

It is your choice.

chapter 12

The Psychology of Confidence

"The first and most important step toward success is the expectation that we can succeed."

Nelson Boswell

Chapter 12

THE PSYCHOLOGY OF CONFIDENCE

The wonderfully named Frank Outlaw is credited with originating the quote which has been attributed in different forms to many others: "Watch your thoughts, they become words; watch your words, they become actions; watch your actions, they become habits; watch your habits, they become character; watch your character, for it becomes your destiny." Isn't that powerful? It invokes the idea of moving from birth to destiny, rather than from birth to death. One thing that winners have – and which is available to all of us – is a sense of destiny.

I also like the way leadership coach John C. Maxwell puts it: "When you change your thinking, you change your beliefs; when you change your beliefs, you change your expectations; when you change your expectations, you change your attitude; when you change your attitude, you change your behaviour; when you change your behaviour, you change your performance; when you change your performance, you change your life."

We generally understand, deep down inside, that when we change our performance, our lives will change, but getting to that point can seem impossible, especially to adults. It can also seem very intimidating and some people stop even daring to hope. That's why breaking it down, beginning with our thoughts, beliefs and expectations – transiting through attitude and behaviour to performance – is so very powerful.

Part of the challenge we face lies in the comfort of the comfort zone. Many people advise you to step outside your comfort zone, but I prefer the imagery of *expanding* your comfort zone. That way, you get to stay in it; it just gets bigger. The real secret is that the comfort zone exists only in our minds, so it is entirely up to us as to how big and comfy it is, how it feels and what it looks like.

CHAPTER 12: THE PSYCHOLOGY OF CONFIDENCE

Would you like to know the single best way to enlarge and re-upholster your comfort zone? It is to stop making excuses. That's right, no more excuses, whether for not taking action at all or for taking action and not doing as well as you would have liked.

> We have all seen the funny T-shirts with various excuses for not riding, and I am the first to admit that I never really liked riding on very windy days. That was my go-to excuse until I was due to have a jumping lesson with an American event rider called Charles Chipp. "It's windy", I said. "Maybe we should just do flat work." Well, that attitude didn't go over well and I got a much needed lecture about rejoicing when conditions at home were less than ideal, because it was an opportunity to practise and therefore know that we could handle whatever elements nature chose to throw at us when we were competing. Instead of thinking, "Oh no, it's windy," I learned to think, "Hooray! It's windy!" Strangely enough, once I made that mental shift, the weather became almost irrelevant. It's one of the greatest favours anyone ever did for me, not only for my horsemanship but because it applies to many other areas of life.

> *Behind the scenes, success requires plenty of old-fashioned hard work.*

From now on, I challenge you to catch yourself making excuses for not taking action! It is not too cold, too hot, too windy, too wet, too dry, too early or too late. Your horse is not too fresh, too stale, too spooky, too laid back. It is not a deal breaker that you don't have an indoor arena or an outdoor arena. Any and all of these statements mean that you are looking for excuses and that is not the attitude of a winner. By all means acknowledge that it might be hot, cold, windy, wet, sloping or whatever, so make the necessary adjustments to your clothing and pace, but be grateful for the challenge and get on with it. Behind the scenes, success requires plenty of old-fashioned hard work.

The other time our random excuse generator really kicks in is at the event. For example: he was shod too recently or he needed reshoeing, the ground was too hard or too soft, the judge doesn't like (insert characteristic of your choice), my horse is afraid of other horses, my boots were killing me, and so on. Making excuses sucks the life out of your potential to succeed whereas owning 'failure' as a learning experience and a pointer to improvement is the key to accepting that you and you alone are responsible for moving towards your goals. Taking responsibility means that by choosing a new response to a given set of circumstances, you can create a new result.

> Here are five of my favourite quotes to inspire and reassure you about the necessity of failures on the way to successes.
>
> *"When we give ourselves permission to fail, we, at the same time, give ourselves permission to excel."* Eloise Ristad
>
> *"Success is stumbling from failure to failure with no loss of enthusiasm."* Winston Churchill
>
> *"The greatest glory in living lies not in never falling, but in rising every time we fall."* Ralph Waldo Emerson
>
> *"Develop success from failures. Discouragement and failure are two of the surest stepping stones to success."* Dale Carnegie
>
> *"I have not failed. I've just found 10,000 ways that won't work."* Thomas A. Edison

TIP ▶ Get comfortable with things not going according to plan. You'll be in good company!

TIP ▶ Note what needs to be improved (idea), deal with it (action), and do better next time (measurable result).

CHAPTER 12: THE PSYCHOLOGY OF CONFIDENCE

> *Manure happens, deal with it!*

We also need to reflect on and learn from what went right. At the end of the day, you may as well focus on what makes you feel good because feeling bad won't change what's over and done with. Manure happens, deal with it! Given that you will encounter challenges irrespective of whether you shoot for the stars or remain focussed on the weeds, you will be better equipped to deal with those challenges if you are pursuing a worthwhile goal and keep your eyes on the prize.

> *"By deliberately opting to pay attention to big and small things that deserve recognition and celebration, I go to sleep with a sense of satisfaction instead of inadequacy. That helps me wake up excited to build on each new day."*
>
> TORY JOHNSON

Acknowledging small wins and emphasising the positive will help to train your brain to think like a winner. To give you some practical examples:

TURN THIS	INTO THIS
My horse is too green	I have the opportunity to mould my horse
My riding area is so rocky	My horse will be tough and surefooted
I am aching all over	My body is adapting as my skills improve
The weather is awful	Yay, I get to wear my new riding raincoat

In his autobiography *Open*, Andre Agassi writes that every tennis match is a metaphor for life. "Points become games become sets become tournaments, and it's all so tightly connected that any point can become the turning point. It reminds me of the way seconds become minutes become hours, and any hour can be our finest. Or darkest. It's our choice."

Kurek Ashley is the author of *How Would Love Respond?* He also coached the Australian women's beach volleyball team of Natalie Cook and Kerri Ann Pottharst to gold medals at the 2000 Olympics. At a lunch I attended, Kurek posed the question, "What have you been telling yourself is impossible?" He contends that we all have the potential to be winners; that success does not discriminate, it's about who is prepared to do a little bit more. It is also about employing the psychology of winning.

> I was intrigued by some of the innovative things Kurek introduced to assist Natalie and Kerri Ann to focus on visualising and therefore creating what they wanted to achieve. In his words, he "got the girls to be gold medallists in advance".
>
> How? He had them buy display cases for their gold medals two years before the Olympics. Their preferred colour for everything from hair brushes to jewellery was gold, they kept gold things in their medal display cases to attract more gold and they even signed autographs as 'gold medal winner' long before the Olympics.
>
> Natalie bought a gold camera, gold toothbrush and wore a gold coin on a gold chain around her neck to symbolise her gold medal. She even went so far as to mock up a gold medal cut from gold paper on her bathroom mirror, so that every time she cleaned her teeth she saw herself wearing a gold medal.
>
> Every day they would practise accepting their medals while the national anthem was playing. And when it all came true after a cliff-hanger of a final, they had the eerie feeling that it was just like they remembered it.

Chapter 12: The Psychology of Confidence

Have you heard it said that the mind does not know the difference between what is real and what is vividly imagined? Natalie Cook and Kerri Ann Pottharst are proof that it works. The moral of the story is to visualise your own victory, work out what will symbolise it for you, put what you want into your mind, reinforce the vision constantly and start believing it.

Anyone can do it. For example, did you know that actor Jim Carrey wrote himself a cheque for ten million dollars before he ever made a movie? Or that inventor Thomas Edison would often announce a new device before he had perfected it?

TIP ▶ Practise visualising the images you want. Before you fall asleep or when you are waking up are good times, but any time is a fine time for visualisation. See yourself and your horse completing your tasks easily and effortlessly, in perfect harmony. Note how you remember everything. Observe with joy how your horse responds to your every command, no matter how subtle.

TIP ▶ For maximum impact, use all your senses. Feel the rein in your hand, the saddle beneath you, the texture of the mane against your knuckles, the horse's movement through your legs and seat, the wind in your face, the sun or rain on your back, the butterflies in your tummy (as they begin to fly in formation). See your beautiful horse, look where you are going, keep an eye on everything else with your peripheral vision. Hear the horse's footfalls; listen to his breathing and any other sounds he makes. Taste the salt on your lips. Smell that wonderful, herbal, horsey smell.

TIP ▶ If you find that difficult to do, begin by imagining that you are developing a video game of the perfect event, competition, outing or whatever. Once you have your scenario, it is easier to build in the detail. For instance, if your dream involves riding on the beach, paint in the colours and textures, add the soundtrack, dial up the smells, tastes and physical sensations and top it off with some emotion! Add a seagull. Make it as realistic as you possibly can.

TIP ▸ Dream it, do it, repeat. Convert those images from your mind into reality. Go and play your video game in real life.

The best part of all this work on your own mind is that your beliefs and attitudes are also communicated to your horse and to other people. Simple changes in what you think can change the way your horse behaves and when you generate enthusiasm for yourself and your horse, others will be enthusiastic about your partnership too. At a subjective level, the judge buys YOU, so enter the ring with confidence.

Ready, willing and keen to compete! Photographer: Jack Pappas

TIP ▸ Get used to building and projecting that winning feeling.

TIP ▸ Reading inspirational biographies and autobiographies or watching inspirational movies can help you to shift your mindset. They don't have to involve horses.

CHAPTER 12: THE PSYCHOLOGY OF CONFIDENCE

Goal Setting

> *"Obstacles are those frightening things we see when we take our eyes off our goals."*
>
> HENRY FORD

The trouble is, setting the goal itself can be an obstacle for some people! I asked Chris Christoff, author of *Goal Setting for People Who Can't Set Goals*, how to deal with this issue. The first step is to get crystal clear about your goal.

> "You have to have a reason why, and you have to ask yourself that question. Then when you get an answer you have to ask yourself the question again until you get the ultimate reason why, because ultimately the reason why has to do something for you. You might say, 'I'm going to save all the starving children in Africa.' Why? 'Well, because it's a humanitarian crisis.' 'But why?' Ultimately it gets down to, 'Because it's something that I will feel better about, that I will associate with.'
>
> It has to be selfish, and I use the word 'selfish' but in a very positive way, because you have to identify with that 'why'. That's one of the things that hold people back. The other half of that is deserving. Do I deserve this? Again, it's a self-development process, and if you can focus on the goal with enough clarity, and if you can use as many senses as possible, you can hear it, see it, touch it, smell it, taste it, all of those things, then as that belief in the goal develops, the deserving also develops.
>
> The next thing is, 'How do I get there?' Find a coach, or find somebody that you know that has at least a level of horsemanship better than you aspire to. Find out how to do it, and then get off your butt and do it."

> *Winners do not do vague and apologetic.*
> *Winners do not seek permission and approval.*

Be concise, bold, ambitious and smart when you set your goals. Not, "Oh wow, I'd like a nice horse and if it's alright and wouldn't seem presumptuous and if other people wouldn't be too jealous and if I could actually get selected then I wouldn't mind winning an individual medal in the Olympic dressage. In fact, just to take part would be fantastic".

No. Winners do not do vague and apologetic. Winners do not seek permission and approval. They do not entertain compromises in advance. A winner says, "My horse and I are going to the Olympics in Tokyo in July–August 2020 where we will win an individual gold medal in the dressage."

Define what you want and write it down. Understand that your 'playing small' does not serve the universe. We are all here to fulfil our potential. Whatever you set out to do, go forward knowing that anything that lights up your soul will benefit others too.

New Zealand Olympian, Sir Mark Todd, voted Rider of the 20th Century by the International Federation for Equestrian Sports. Here he is looking focussed at Achselschwang, Bavaria, 1998. Photographer: Joanne Verikios

CHAPTER 12: THE PSYCHOLOGY OF CONFIDENCE

TIP ▶ Begin with your personal ideal, saying to yourself, "Assuming there are no obstacles, what do I really want?" Where will you be, where will you ride, what skills will you have, what will your horse look like, how will he behave?

As Chris says, the more vividly you can describe this, the better you will be able to implement it. Remember that Rome wasn't built in a day, and that it's okay to revise your plans and goals as you go along. You might find that your dreams of Olympic gold are replaced by a completely different vision – it happens! The next step is to pencil in your timeframe. If your goal is the Olympics, then which Olympics? And how far away is that? Once you have your big, dream goal before you in writing, you can add structure by developing and refining all the short, medium and long term goals along the way.

Now you need a strategy. What is that? Who do you need on your team? At this point, depending on your aspirations, you may need to cast your net wider than the immediate horse world. Think finance brokers, sponsors, your family, employer, employees, and business colleagues.

Never be afraid to think big. The people who achieve big goals are just like you and me, with horses just like yours and mine. If they can do it, you can do it. The reason they make it happen is that they have a laser focus on the desired outcome, they believe in themselves (and their team), they believe in their horse, they proceed as if they cannot fail, they are resilient when they do fail, they take massive action and they create the future they want.

So let's say we have our sights set on a big goal like reaching the moon. I believe it was Neil Armstrong who said they faced only two problems with putting a man on the moon. The first was how to get there. The second was how to get back. It was very important to have the second problem solved before leaving home!

Unlike that first moonwalk, when it comes to equestrian excellence many others have been there already, so we have a trail to follow. We even know the rocket ships that work best and all the steps that lead up to the final countdown before blast off. We know what we need to wear, what food to pack for zero gravity, the road we must take to get to the launch site. All we have to do is document those steps, inventories and routes, do the training, buy the supplies and we are on our way. It is that simple, and that difficult.

The key is to have a plan. Let's face it, most people put more time and effort into planning their next holiday than into planning their lives, but you don't have to be one of them. As an extension of your goals, you must learn to create tactical plans that detail how your short, medium and long-range goals will be achieved. Not starting is guaranteed failure. Giving up is guaranteed failure. But commit, begin, see it through and you are on the way to success.

TIP ▶ Make your goal even more tangible and measurable by anchoring it in something you can experience with one or more of your senses, just like Natalie Cook and Kerri Ann Pottharst did.

> *"It's the chance of a lifetime, in a lifetime of chance. And it's high time you joined in the dance."*
>
> DAN FOGELBERG

Believe me, when you set a goal that resonates with the very depths of your soul, you will not stop until you have reached it. Surround yourself with the types of people who will help you to succeed and structure your life to increase your effectiveness at whatever it is you want to achieve. Once you put the wheels in motion, if you maintain consistency and dedication, you will inevitably begin to experience more and more success. Your vision, goals, plans, attitude and the environment you create will help you to surmount obstacles and ultimately achieve your goals. If you are clear, decisive, committed and set milestones and deadlines, you will manifest what you want. You will find a way.

In "Run for the Roses", Dan Fogelberg sings: "It's the chance of a lifetime, in a lifetime of chance. And it's high time you joined in the dance."

It's high time you joined in the dance. So, what is your dance?

chapter 13

Present – It's Showtime!

"Perfection is not attainable, but if we chase perfection we can catch excellence."

Vince Lombardi

chapter 13
Present – It's Showtime!

The big day has arrived. You have equipped, nourished, nurtured, conditioned, educated and prepared both yourself and your horse. You have goals and plans. You have worked on your mindset. Congratulations! Now you are ready to present the fruits of your combined labours to the world, and to do so with confidence.

Many years ago, I was lucky enough to take part in a business-oriented workshop with a remarkable trainer. I regret that I have forgotten his name or I would gladly give him credit. The focus was presentation skills but the course covered much more than that. It was at this course that I was introduced to the concept of living above or below the line; in essence choosing whether to take responsibility and be accountable or make excuses and lay blame elsewhere.

> *"If you know how to be bad, you know how to be good".*

The first thing the trainer did was ask us each to get up in front of the class and give the worst presentation we possibly could. Of course we all excelled at this, exaggerating our nervousness, deliberately thinking up mistakes to make and having a good time in the process. "There you have it," said the trainer, "you don't need this course". Someone was brave enough to ask why and I will never forget the answer: "If you know how to be bad, you know how to be good". You just need to turn the tables on the voice telling you that you can't do it, and listen to the voice that says you can. Connect it to a trigger phrase and you have the foundations of a successful performance. So simple and so effective.

Since that day, whenever I have been about to perform in any capacity, whether public speaking, exhibiting a horse or lifting a big weight in

CHAPTER 13: PRESENT – IT'S SHOWTIME!

front of a World Championships crowd, I have recalled his teaching and used my chosen phrase: "It's showtime!"

"It's showtime!"

Joanne Verikios with the then Mr ACT, Stan Hambesis, in a publicity shot prior to the 1987 Women's World Powerlifting Championships. Photo credit: Fairfax Media/Fairfax Syndication

TIP ▶ Find a psych-up phrase that works for you and use it. The more you do so with consistency and conviction, the easier it gets. You can even say it to your horse when you want him to perform. He will soon learn what it means.

Using your trigger phrase will help you to look confident, not apologetic. The image you want to project is that you are completely in love with this horse and that you firmly believe he or she is the best animal there. As Yoda says, "Do or do not. There is no try".

The Wow Factor

You have done your training and preparation. You and your horse are well-groomed, fit and clean. Now for the finishing touches that ensure you have a great day – if you get them right.

Compliance

All your gear looks terrific, but have you also made sure that it is legal for your event? Are spurs allowed? If so, do yours match the criteria? Are whips allowed? If so, does yours measure up? What kinds of bridles or bits or nosebands are allowed? Do yours comply? Is your girth sufficient or is a surcingle also required? Are you allowed to use a martingale or a breastplate or a crupper? Do you have the protective clothing and headgear specified in the rules? You do not want to be running around trying to beg, borrow or buy replacement equipment on the day of the event; nor do you want to waste all your hard work and your entry fees by being disqualified.

In some instances, horses must be presented for competition without boots, bandages or eventing grease; in other events such protection is very common. It is also your responsibility to ensure that items that might be allowed in the warm-up arena are removed before you compete, if that is what the rules require. If you are lucky, a steward or a friend might remind you to take off your bandages or drop your whip or whatever the case may be, but the ultimate responsibility for compliance lies with you.

CHAPTER 13: PRESENT – IT'S SHOWTIME!

TIP ▶ Know the rules. Abide by the rules.

To Plait or Not to Plait

There are many ways to present your horse's tail and mane at showtime, from *au naturel* to pulled, plaited, banded or braided; hogged and taped like a polo pony; or beribboned and decorated with flowers, ears of wheat and bells like a draught horse. Much depends on the event and the breed. After that, it's down to your own skills, time available and personal preferences.

> During the 2015 Australian Warmblood Horse Association Assessment Tour, Silvia Ahamer demonstrated how a plaited tail can constrict a horse's movement – a revelation for the owners and a godsend for several horses when their tails were set free!
>
> In their guidelines, the AWHA actually recommends that tails not be plaited and that plaits, if used, be loose. Nevertheless, some people did present their horses plaited up to the nines, which let us see quite a few before and afters because everybody accepted our suggestion to un-plait. I remember a ridden mare who held her tail clamped down and to one side with it plaited. Then you could see her centring her tail and relaxing her back when the plaits came out and suddenly she moved a whole lot better.
>
> It made me uneasy to think of all the tails I have plaited in the past. I probably even wondered why the poor horse "didn't go as well as he did at home". These days, I would definitely opt for other methods of neatening the top of the tail if required, or simply accept that horses have tails and it is alright to present them in all their glory.

TIP ▶ If you opt to plait, always ease the dock into its natural curve when you have finished. Taking thicker sections of tail may be more comfortable for the horse than the very fine strands that are often seen. Think basket weave rather than birdcage.

If the mane is to be plaited, it is customary to have an uneven number of plaits along the neck. The forelock is usually plaited but may be left loose for most events. Manes may not have such a big effect on movement because the spacing of the plaits allows for flexion of the neck, but I am sure that if some hairs were pulling badly it could impact on a horse's attitude, so do not plait so tightly.

A pulled mane...Photographer: Jeanne O'Malley

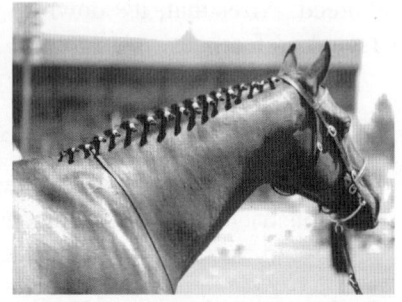

...is easier to plait. Photographer: Jeanne O'Malley

TIP ▶ Experiment ahead of time with all your grooming enhancements, including how many and what kind of plaits you will have, then stick to your plan on show day.

> *If makeup is allowed, remember that you want to enhance your horse, not disguise him.*

Polish

A show sheen product will add extra gloss to your horse. It will also make him slippery, so keep it away from behind the ears and avoid the saddle and girth area of a riding horse. If makeup is allowed, remember that you want to enhance your horse, not disguise him. Please also consider his comfort – a lot of oil-based product on his skin on a hot day may set him up for sunburn or eye irritation.

CHAPTER 13: PRESENT – IT'S SHOWTIME!

TIP ▶ Hair spray can help to keep your plaits and quarter marks in place.

TIP ▶ A little equine fly spray, applied first to a cloth and then carefully wiped on, will keep him from being annoyed by insect pests and help to keep him settled.

Hooves and chestnuts may be oiled or painted with the hoof product of your choice, depending on (a) any rules and (b) whatever fashion might apply. An old trick to subtly enhance the hooves is to use boot polish. Select an appropriate colour, such as neutral for white feet. Apply carefully with a rag wrapped around your finger and buff well. Include the back of the hoof, the frog and the chestnuts inside the knees and hocks for a harmonious look.

TIP ▶ If you decide to use hoof oil, make sure you rub it right off again, so the feet look moist but not greasy. There are two reasons for this. One is that excess oil will attract dust, making the hoof and coronet look dull and grubby. The second is that the judge may want to inspect your horse's foot and he or she does not want to get grease and dust on their hands when they pick it up.

TIP ▶ When using hoof polish, spray the hooves with hair spray just prior to entering the ring. It will remove dust or scuff marks and add shine.

TIP ▶ To avoid soreness, do not get your horse's feet trimmed or new shoes put on within three days of an important event.

Looking the Part

Your own presentation should also be high on the agenda when preparing for a show. A beautifully groomed horse presented by a neat, tidy, competent handler or rider will tend to catch the judge's eye for the right reasons.

Posture

"Come on kids! Stand up straight! Head up, chest out, stomach in!" I am so grateful that my parents trained us to adopt good posture as a default. The first thing the judge will notice about you is your bearing, in other words, your poise and posture. Holding your body in proper alignment, with all of the components in balance from top to bottom, side to side and front to back is good for you in a number of ways.

Firstly, it prevents muscle strain and tension, because, with everything stacked properly, there is little need for effort to keep things in place and movement is more efficient. Secondly, with your chest open and spine elongated, there is plenty of room for your lungs to expand, for your diaphragm to do its thing and for your digestive organs to work without compression. Thirdly, it makes us look stronger, slimmer and more confident. So smile, sit or stand tall and look the world in the eye!

TIP ▸ Be conscious of your posture, sitting, standing, moving and riding and correct it often.

What to Wear and How to Wear It

Winners need skill backed up by training and preparation, but it definitely helps with first impressions and your own confidence if you have a winning look, so know the rules and think carefully when putting together your attire for competition.

Tradition plays a big part in the equestrian world and tradition has usually stood the test of time because it is durable and functional. You want to send a clear message to the judge and your competition that you are a serious contender, that you know what you are doing and that you belong in the class. The more successful a rider is, the more polish and professionalism they seem to exude. This is a combination of both equipment and knowhow. Even the way you wear your hat can make a difference.

Not so many decades ago, the only women wearing skirts in the show ring would have been judges and those skirts would have been long and

CHAPTER 13: PRESENT – IT'S SHOWTIME!

full, perhaps even divided riding skirts – a throwback to the days of side saddles. The competitors, whether they rode or led, would all have worn traditional English, Western or stockman's riding attire, with the exception that competitors in led classes usually wore footwear more suitable for running than leather-soled boots. Why was that? For one thing, in all but equitation and turnout classes, the horse was on show, not the exhibitor. For another, tradition was king and conservatism was queen. The traditional garb of horsemen and horsewomen around the world stems from long experience and an inherent desire for functionality, protection and modesty.

Philip III of France, who reigned from 1270–1285, was known as 'Le Hardi' (The Bold) on the basis of his abilities in combat and on horseback.

Now, especially in non-Western breed classes, novelty rules, skirts are almost the norm for women, and footwear varies from the practical to the suicidal. Call me old-fashioned but in my view, as a judge, I believe that handler attire in led classes has become too diverse and sometimes not suitable for the purpose or conditions. For example, if you need to run with a horse in deep going and/or hot, windy conditions, fashion outfits will not do your mobility or comfort any favours.

> Let us picture an entrant in a led class. The horse, fit as a trout, is gleaming, plaited and polished to the hilt. The handler is wearing an outfit worthy of Fashions on the Field, from picture hat and fitted skirt to ballet flats. They undoubtedly present an eye-catching picture. They begin their workout. At the walk, the horse wants to go but the handler discovers that her skirt is not designed for striding out. At the trot, the horse throws his head around a bit and off comes her hat. Momentarily flustered, the handler takes a firmer grip on the lead rein. This gives the horse the leverage he needs to reef his head up, pulling the handler's blouse out of her waistband on the way. Her weight makes the horse wobble to the left, bumping her so she stumbles and falls. Fortunately she is unhurt but her dignity has suffered from revealing more than originally intended to the judge and spectators.

You want your outfit for a led class to enhance safety, decorum and enable you to RUN without restraint, just as an outfit for a ridden class should enhance safety, decorum and allow you to RIDE without getting your legs pinched or having lots of fabric flapping around. You may indeed be able to run in a stretch skirt or a full skirt, but what if you fall? These things happen. You may think you can run in ballet flats or kitten heels, but have you tried it on slippery grass or when your shoes are full of arena sand or wood chips? And what protection do they offer if your horse – or someone else's horse – steps on your foot? One of the advantages of boots and closed shoes is that they have a layer or two of protection between hoof and instep.

Judges prefer to see workmanlike attire that is both elegant and functional. I do not think you can go wrong wearing whatever riding

CHAPTER 13: PRESENT – IT'S SHOWTIME!

apparel is currently stylish and appropriate to the breed you are exhibiting, save that you must choose footwear you can run in, perhaps rubber riding boots or riding sneakers. Weather permitting, men will always look correct in a shirt and tie with suit coat or waistcoat.

> *As in the boardroom, the more skin you show the less authority you project.*
>
> JOANNE VERIKIOS

For less formal led events such as at classification days and assessment tours, you may wish to consider adopting the current European convention of polo shirt or long-sleeved shirt, long pants and running shoes; with an optional hat or helmet. Jeans tend not to look professional enough for showing, but moleskins, chinos and bowling or cricket-flannel type trousers can work. As in the boardroom, the more skin you show the less authority you project. Match the calibre of outfit to the formality and prestige of the event but always keep it smart, practical, neat and comfortable.

Christopher Ardron, a Warmblood breeder, international classifier and dressage judge, agrees. According to Christopher, men showing horses in hand should wear shirts in their stud colours or plain white. If your breed association has a logo shirt, then that could also be a good choice. He does not want to see sweat rings under the arms and shirts not tucked in. For women, Christopher suggests taking inspiration from the elegantly dressed ladies who wear a pant suit or a skirt suit to run out dogs at dog shows. If skirts are worn, they should be a sensible length and teamed with stockings and simple shoes that are smart, comfortable and flat-heeled. Everything should be clean, ironed and well fitted. Nothing should be 'over the top'.

TIP ▶ Long hair should be restrained in a bun or pony tail. If you wear a riding cap, then a hair net is also correct for longer hair and no hair should show on your forehead.

TIP ▶ If you wear a tie, either keep your jacket fastened or use a tie pin so that the tie doesn't fly up into your or the horse's face.

TIP ▶ Watch as many events of the kind you want to compete in as you can, preferably live, so you can focus on those subtle details and carefully observe what the winners are wearing and how they wear it.

TIP ▶ If your horse has white legs, wear dark pants; if he has dark legs, wear light pants. Similarly, choose a shirt, blouse or coat colour that will frame his head without clashing with it or matching it.

TIP ▶ Invest in getting your colours done by a professional colour consultant and take along a colour photograph of your horse. It will give you one of those unfair advantages in the ring and over time it will save you a fortune because you will never again buy something that doesn't suit you or go with anything else in your wardrobe.

TIP ▶ A pair of overalls will keep your show outfit pristine until you remove them just before you compete.

TIP ▶ Always clean your horse's tack and your own clothing a few days in advance and have a dress rehearsal so there is time for repairs or to purchase missing items.

TIP ▶ Always pack the night before.

TIP ▶ Always use checklists.

Count Your Blessings

A big part of a winning attitude is forgiveness. Forgive your horse for not being perfect – the perfect horse exists only in the imagination. Forgive yourself for not being perfect – perfect humans are even less common than perfect horses. On occasion, you may have to forgive the judge for not recognising your perfection. Forgive the world around you

CHAPTER 13: PRESENT – IT'S SHOWTIME!

for not being perfect. We and our horses must learn to live in the world as we find it, not as we would like it to be. Forgive other people for not being perfect. To a greater or lesser extent, they too are doing the best they can with what they have.

> *"Peace is the result of retraining your mind to process life as it is, rather than as you think it should be."*
>
> WAYNE W. DYER

You will probably find that it helps to practise forgiveness on at least a daily basis. A nice little ritual you might like to try goes like this: When you first wake up, just lie in bed for a few moments. Then send 'a day of loving kindness' to several people – just whoever comes into your mind, whether you even like them or not. Then, silently practise gratitude for everything you have. Next, practise forgiveness, using the above suggestions or any opportunities for being forgiving that may have cropped up in the last day or so. Finally, give yourself a hug of love and approval.

Some successful entrepreneurs go for a 'gratitude walk' every day. As they exercise and breathe in the fresh air, they think of something for which to be grateful beginning with every letter of the alphabet. It works beautifully when you are riding too. Try it as a relaxing and joyful way to warm up for a training session or begin a trail ride.

Me riding Dots and George riding Missy at 8,000 feet, Grand Teton Mountain Range, Wyoming 2012. Photographer unknown

We really do live in a wonderful world and it is important to acknowledge the abundance that we often take for granted in the course of our busy lives and inevitable disappointments. Just thinking about how blessed we are to enjoy the company of horses and the means to keep them helps us to stay grounded and appreciative.

Form a clear intention of the kind of day, ride, training session you are going to have; do your best and make the most of whatever comes. Love, gratitude, forgiveness, empathy and self-approval are a powerful combination!

Let us conclude with our formula from the first chapter: Consistency Communicates, Persistence Pays, Dreams Develop and Vision Vitalises.

CC + PP + DD + VV = WINNING

May you and your horse have fun, winning, together.

Author's Final Word

If you can maintain your passion, build your confidence and skills, and enhance your knowledge and wisdom, you will have achieved something significant and important – a personal achievement with the far reaching benefit of becoming a better friend to all horses.

From Misery to Mastery
by
Joanne Verikios

Did you try force

And regret losing your head?

Perhaps he was punished,

Or you just wished he was dead?

Many have been there

Through their pride and their ego.

But that kind of pride

Is not our amigo!

Instead be so patient

And take enough time.

You'll get there much faster

And your lessons will rhyme!

When you can relate to your horse

Soul to soul, book to shelf,

There'll be no more remorse

For you'll have mastered yourself.

-oOOo-

Many people have helped me over the years. In turn, I sincerely hope I have helped you and I encourage you to pay it forward, share and help others.

Please stay in touch and keep up-to-date with events, resources and recommended products by visiting www.WinningHorsemanship.com on a regular basis.

About the Author

JOANNE VERIKIOS

Joanne Verikios is an accomplished author, trusted health and lifestyle consultant, experienced horse breeder and trainer, award-winning athlete, and successful real estate investor.

Having received her first pony at the age of nine, Joanne's earliest ambition in life was to be a bareback horse rider in a circus. Although she never ran off to join the circus, after working her way through the Pony Club ranks, she earned the qualification of Pony Club instructor at the age of sixteen. One of the many highlights of her early riding career was being a member of the Downs Pony Club team that won the Duke of Edinburgh Pony Club Games Championship in 1972.

While working at the Australian Public Service, Joanne qualified for an Australian Owner Trainer Permit to train and race Thoroughbreds. She also pursued her love of horses by founding the Highborn Warmblood Stud, where she was Stud Manager for sixteen years. The horses Joanne bred went on to win both under saddle and in breed classes, including Royal Show Championships. They included the stallion, Highborn Powerlifter, who passed Colt Selection and Performance Testing with flying colours.

In addition to serving on several horse sport committees and officiating at many shows and events, Joanne is a past Federal President and Federal Registrar of the Australian Warmblood Horse Association, which she continues to serve as a Classifier and Classifier Trainer, Judge and Judge Trainer and National Assessment Tour Australian representative. In recognition of her outstanding contribution and commitment to the Association for over 30 years, Joanne was granted Honorary Life membership in 2015.

Joanne was also an Australian Powerlifting Champion, holding State, National, and Commonwealth records. Twice, Joanne represented Australia at the Women's World Powerlifting Championships and was ranked seventh in the world both times. In peak condition, Joanne was able to deadlift more than triple her bodyweight. Her feats of strength are recorded in the 1989 and 1991 Guinness Book of Records with Australian Supplement.

Joanne has published articles in many equine publications including Hoofbeats, Horsezone, Horses & People, The Horse Magazine, Australian Horse and Rider Yearbook, and Hoofs & Horns. She has also published articles in several recreational and sports magazines, including Bellydance Oasis, SPORTZlife, and The Pump.

Joanne lives in Queensland, Australia.

Recommended Resources

Recommended Resources

Giddyupgirl Equestrian Fashion

Contact Giddyupgirl

07 5449 9808 (+61 7 5449 9808)

info@giddyupgirl.com.au

www.giddyupgirl.com.au

PO Box 1787, Noosa Heads, QLD 4567, Australia

Designed by Riders for Riders.

Recommended Resources

Evidence Based Worming

EBW
evidencebasedworming.com.au

Jude Matusiewicz
0410 527 745 (+61 410 527 745)
info@evidencebasedworming.com.au
www.evidencebasedworming.com.au
Confirm *BEFORE* You Worm.

Jude Matusiewicz has kindly offered a **FREE BONUS GIFT** valued at $50.00 to all readers of this book…

Lifecycle of a Cyathostomin (Small Strongyle) e-Poster. This poster can be printed out in A3 and laminated for a long wall life. Not just a lifecycle diagram, it contains many fascinating facts and insights about Cyathostomins. It is in full colour and fully referenced.

Simply visit the website below and follow the directions to claim your poster.

www.WinningHorsemanship.com/gifts

Muddy Creek Rain Gear

Dianne Denton

0429 995 596 (+61 429 995 596)

dianne@muddycreekraingear.com.au

www.muddycreekraingear.com.au

209 Diamond Beach Road, Diamond Beach, NSW 2430, Australia

The Ultimate Riding Rain Gear –
Ultra Lightweight, Waterproof, Breathable.

Recommended Resources

Hay Maximizers

Dianne Denton

0429 995 596 (+61 429 995 596)

dianne@haymaximizer.com.au

www.haymaximizer.com.au

209 Diamond Beach Road, Diamond Beach, NSW 2430, Australia

Slow Feed Hay Bags designed by an Australian Equine Natural Therapist, to benefit you, your horse and your wallet!

Beach Holidays with Your Horse

SEAHORSE
of Diamond Beach

Contact Chris

0467 489 975 (+61 467 489 975)

holiday@seahorsediamondbeach.com.au

www.seahorsediamondbeach.com.au

Diamond Beach, NSW 2430, Australia

Bring Your Horse on Holidays Too. Unique horse-and-dog-friendly, quality beach holiday accommodation.

WINNING™
HORSEMANSHIP